PIR TES
TREASURES
Facts · Feats · Firsts
IN PITTSBURGH PIRATES HISTORY

ON THE COVER:
Upper left - Roberto Clemente
Upper middle - Honus Wagner
Upper right - Bob Robertson, Willie Stargell
Lower left - Hall of Fame Pitcher Pud Galvin
Lower middle - Exposition Park
Lower right - Pie Traynor

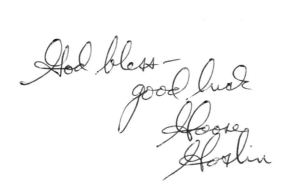

God bless —
good luck
Posey
Hoslin

PIRATES
TREASURES

By Bob Fulton

Published by Golden Goose Enterprises, Inc.
Printed by Geyer Printing Co., Pittsburgh
Cover design by Giuseppe Francioni, Prisma, Inc., Pittsburgh
© 1999 Golden Goose Enterprises, Inc.

ISBN 0-9675715-0-2

PREFACE

I became a fan of the Pittsburgh Pirates the day my father first took me to a game at Forbes Field. I can't say I recall any particulars—just that he stood up at one point, barehanded a foul pop and calmly handed me the ball. His ho-hum demeanor after the catch contrasted with my wide-eyed expression. Yes, I became a fan of the Pirates that day and I've been a student of the team ever since. Much of the knowledge I've accumulated in the years since has been poured into *Pirates Treasures*. This is no ordinary trivia book, focused solely on records and statistics. I favor the offbeat, the colorful, the humorous, even the bizarre. You'll read about the doubleheader completed underwater; the indoor game that was rained out; the player who died after drinking seawater; and the rookie who struck out while sitting on the bench. You'll read about the publicity director who "won" the Bucs a game; the outfielders whose pursuit of a batted ball was interrupted by a gun-toting Cincinnati fan; the throng of 50,000 that jammed downtown streets for a Pirates game that wasn't even played in Pittsburgh; the loyal fan who vowed he wouldn't shave until the Bucs won the pennant; and the tipsy Pirates pitcher who fell asleep during a game at Ebbets Field—inside the tarp.

I cover every facet of the team's history in *Pirates Treasures*: the players, managers, coaches, owners, P.A. announcers, mascots, trainers, ballparks, broadcasters, organists . . . even angels (the ones who intervened to help the lowly Pirates win a pennant in a classic 1951 movie). You'll learn which Pittsburgh broadcaster succeeded a future United States president; why a sparrow flew from beneath Casey Stengel's cap during a 1918 game; what prompted a Pirates center fielder to turn his back on baseball and become the Billy Graham of his day; and how a Pittsburgh outfielder "caught" his own home run ball.

In a sense, the inspiration for *Pirates Treasures* was a long-ago afternoon at Forbes Field when a father introduced his son to the Bucs and even caught a foul ball to mark the occasion. I still

1

have the baseball. And I still have a sense of wide-eyed wonder about the team I've followed ever since.

ABOUT THE AUTHOR

Bob Fulton has written extensively about the Pittsburgh Pirates for *The Indiana Gazette* and national and regional publications such as *Sports History, Pittsburgh Magazine, The National Pastime, Pennsylvania* and *On Deck*, the official magazine of the Pirates. His work has also appeared in *American Heritage, Football Digest, The NCAA News, NFL Exclusive, Delta Sky, Basketball Weekly, Referee, The Elks Magazine, International Gymnast* and *Sports Heritage*. Fulton is the author of *The Summer Olympics: A Treasury of Legend and Lore; Never Lost a Game (Time Just Ran Out)*; and *Top Ten Baseball Stats: Interesting Rankings of Players, Managers, Umpires and Teams*. A graduate of Indiana University of Pennsylvania, he resides in Indiana.

ACKNOWLEDGEMENTS

The author would like to express his gratitude to fellow members of the Society for American Baseball Research, who cheerfully provided information on a wide range of topics; the helpful and knowledgeable staff at the National Baseball Hall of Fame and Library in Cooperstown, N.Y.; the Pittsburgh Pirates, for granting permission to reprint all photographs used in the book; Jim Trdinich, Ben Bouma and Mike Kennedy, members of the Pirates media relations staff, for their expert assistance; former media relations assistant and current alumni liaison Sally O'Leary, for graciously accepting whatever challenge was tossed her way; and Pirates players, managers and coaches, past and present, who were so generous with their time.

DEDICATION

To my late father, Wayne Fulton, who worked as an usher at Forbes Field and Three Rivers Stadium for more than 40 years and passed on to his son a passion for the Pirates and baseball in general.

ABOUT THIS BOOK

There are several points to keep in mind while reading *Pirates Treasures*:

1. For a period of 20-plus years sandwiching the turn of the century, the "h" was dropped from Pittsburgh. Newspaper names and references to Pittsburgh in newspaper accounts from those years reflect that fact.

2. Team nicknames reflect contemporary, not current, usage. For example, the Pirates opposed the Boston Pilgrims in the 1903 World Series; the Red Sox nickname was not adopted until four years later.

3. The modern era, as defined here, began in 1900.

4. Where source books disagree on statistical matters—especially figures from the 19th century that, because of continuing research, have been revised—the author relied on *Total Baseball*.

5. Information is current as of Sept. 1, 1999.

Q Fred Carroll slugged the first home run in Pirates history on May 2, 1887, helping Pittsburgh dispatch Detroit, 8-3. But his feat was overshadowed by something that took place 48 hours earlier. What?

A In perhaps the most bizarre Opening Day ceremony in baseball history, Carroll buried his beloved pet monkey beneath home plate prior to his team's 6-2 victory over Chicago.

That oddball interment didn't move Pirates fans nearly as much as Carroll's home run. "The excitement among the crowd was of the wildest kind," noted the *Pittsburgh Post*. "Hats were thrown into the air and men and women cheered wildly."

Carroll received something other than applause for his historic home run. According to a painstakingly thorough *Post* account, Gusky and Co. presented him with a silk hat, size 7⅞.

Q The first batter in the very first Pirates game later gained worldwide acclaim—but not for his baseball exploits. Name this Chicago outfielder.

A Evangelist Billy Sunday.

Before devoting his life to saving souls, Sunday was employed as a "baseballist," to use a popular 19th-century term. As the leadoff man for the Chicago White Stockings on April 30, 1887, he was the game's first batter when the Bucs made their National League debut. Sunday pounded out two hits that day.

A player of modest ability (.248 career average, 12 home runs), Sunday would achieve infinitely greater success as an evangelist than he ever did during his eight major league seasons, three of which (1888-1890) were spent with the Pirates.

The turning point in Sunday's life came in Chicago, while he was sitting with several teammates on a curbstone, listening to a revivalist preacher. He supposedly turned to his companions and said, "Boys, I bid the old life goodbye."

Sunday became the Billy Graham of his day, preaching to an estimated 100 million people during his 40-year ministry.

Q Who was the Pirates' first batter in their debut game?

A Left fielder Abner Dalrymple, a former Chicago teammate of Sunday's. Dalrymple tripled leading off the bottom of the first and scored the first run in Pirates history when Tommy Brown followed with a single.

Q Which player spent more seasons in a Pirates uniform than any other?

A Willie Stargell, with 21. Stargell came up in September of 1962 and retired following the 1982 season, 2,360 games later. Only Roberto Clemente (2,433) and Honus Wagner (2,432) played in more as Pirates.

Stargell later served as a coach for one season (1985) under Chuck Tanner. He now serves as a special assistant to general manager Cam Bonifay.

"THEY WON WITH GUNS"

T hat was the headline in the *Pittsburg Commercial Gazette* following what was possibly the zaniest episode in Pirates history.

Pittsburgh left fielder Elmer Smith and center fielder Jake Stenzel were "held up" by an armed fan while pursuing a ball hit by Cincinnati's George "Germany" Smith at League Park on July 20, 1894. While the two Pirates were thus occupied, Smith gleefully circled the bases with a game-winning home run.

"The day began with a ballgame as advertised, but before that contest was over all kinds of outdoor sports were introduced, and the unexpected features were greatly appreciated by the howling spectators," noted the *Commercial Gazette*. "There were wrestling matches, catch-as-catch can, rough-and-tumble fights, a display of firearms and a life-like imitation of a riot in which two of Pittsburg's best and most popular players were assigned the role of victims."

The lunacy began in the 10th inning after Cincinnati's Farmer Vaughn slugged a solo home run to tie the game, 6-6.

"A second later pandemonium reigned," noted the *Commercial Gazette*. "Germany Smith caught a low one full on the nose. It went sailing on a line for the left field seats."

The ball clattered around in the bleachers, which were in play according to the ground rules. When Elmer Smith hopped the fence and reached down to retrieve the ball, a half-dozen "husky occupants" fell on him and tried to wrestle the ball away. Stenzel raced to Smith's rescue, but by then more fans had become involved. That's when the spectator drew a gun.

"Fred Benzinger, a well-known citizen, jumped into the fray," the Commercial Gazette reported. "Stenzel called him a vile name, it is said, and in the midst of the melee Benzinger went for his gun. The appearance of a weapon acted as magic in stopping the fight." Unfortunately for the Pirates, Germany Smith had by then crossed home plate with the run that gave Cincinnati a 7-6 victory.

Q The Pirates' history as a National League franchise dates to 1887. But the team actually originated as a member of what other major league?

A The American Association. Pittsburgh was granted a charter franchise in the Association, which operated from 1882 through 1891. The upstarts challenged the more-established National League by charging only 25 cents admission (half the NL standard), playing Sunday games and permitting the sale of beer at concession stands.

Pittsburgh defeated the eventual champion Cincinnati Red Stockings 10-9 at Cincinnati's Bank Street Grounds on May 2, 1882, in the Association's first contest. A one-paragraph report in the *Pittsburgh Post* noted that "the game was characterized by heavy hitting on both sides. The visitors outfielded the local team and won the contest on their merits." Center fielder Charlie Morton went 4-for-5 with a triple and right fielder Ed Swartwood and third baseman Billy Taylor cracked home runs to back winning pitcher Jack Leary.

The Pittsburgh club wound up fourth (39-39) in the American Association's inaugural season and finished as high as second—albeit 12 games behind champion St. Louis—in 1886, its final year of membership. The Pirates joined the National League along with Indianapolis after the Kansas City and St. Louis franchises were dropped at the urging of the National League's eastern clubs, who groused about traveling costs to such remote (by 19th-century standards) western outposts.

Pittsburgh's first National League team in 1887 was dominated by players who had performed for the city's American Association club the year before.

Q How many other major league teams have called Pittsburgh home?

A Three. The Union Association, which had a one-year run (1884), placed one of its franchises in Pittsburgh (the Stogies), as did the Players League (the Burghers), which observed its birth—and demise—in 1890.

6

Finally, the Federal League located a club (the Rebels) in Pittsburgh both years (1914-15) of its existence.

Q When the Pirates entered the National League in 1887, they were known by a different nickname. What?

A The Alleghenys, derived from the name of the town in which the team played its games. Allegheny was later incorporated into the city of Pittsburgh as the present-day North Side.

The team didn't adopt its current nickname until the 1891 season.

For clarity's sake, Pittsburgh's National League club of 1887-1890 will be recognized as the Pirates in all subsequent references.

Q How many major league teams have used their nickname longer, on a continuous basis?

A Only one. The New York franchise, which is now located in San Francisco, adopted the Giants nickname after manager Jim Mutrie popularized it in 1885. They had previously been known as the Gothams. First baseman Roger Connor, at 6-3, 220 pounds a giant of a man for that era, supposedly inspired the new nickname.

The only other nicknames older than the Pirates still in use are the Reds of Cincinnati and the Phillies of Philadelphia, which both date to 1890. However, both teams went to other nicknames for a time.

The Cincinnati club adopted Redlegs as its nickname in 1953, the midst of the McCarthy era, because Reds had Communist overtones. Cincinnati restored its old nickname in 1959. The Phils adopted Blue Jays as their nickname in 1944 at the behest of new president Bob Carpenter Jr., who held a name-the-team contest that drew 5,064 entries. But by 1946, Phillies was back in vogue.

After the Giants and Pirates, the oldest continuous nicknames are the Cardinals (in use since 1900), Tigers (1901), Athletics (1901), Cubs (1902), White Sox (1904) and Red Sox (1907).

Q How did the Pirates acquire their nickname?

A The Bucs were accused of stealing second baseman Lou Bierbauer from the Philadelphia Athletics of the American Association.

Like many other big leaguers, Bierbauer had jumped to the fledgling Players League in 1890 (he signed with Brooklyn). When the Players League disbanded after only one season, the players were ordered to return to their 1889 clubs.

Bierbauer defied that directive. When the Athletics inadvertently left him off their reserve list, which bound players to their respective teams, he declared himself a free agent and signed with Pittsburgh. The Athletics and the other AA clubs were outraged and accused the Alleghenys of "piratical" actions. But Pittsburgh kept Bierbauer—and the nickname.

Q Of what significance are the dates April 17, 1955, and Oct. 11, 1972, in Pirates history?

A They marked the first and last games of outfielder Roberto Clemente's Hall of Fame career.

Clemente went 3-for-8 with a double against the Dodgers as the Bucs dropped a doubleheader at Forbes Field on April 17, 1955. He sat out the first three games of the season—manager Fred Haney started rookie Roman Mejias in right field—before making his debut. Clemente smashed an infield single off the glove of shortstop Pee Wee Reese in his first at bat, against Johnny Podres.

"The Great One" made his final appearance in a Pirates uniform on Oct. 11, 1972, when Pittsburgh lost Game 5 of the National League Championship Series at Cincinnati's Riverfront Stadium. Clemente was 1-for-3 and drew an intentional walk from Tom Hall in his last trip to the plate.

Q Which Pirates pitcher threw no-hit ball—perfect ball, in fact—longer than anyone in major league history?

A Harvey Haddix, who handcuffed the Milwaukee Braves for 12 innings on May 26, 1959, at County Stadium in what a Pittsburgh newspaper described as "the greatest game ever pitched." Haddix lost his no-hitter—and the game—in the 13th.

Only later, when he was surrounded by reporters in the locker room, did Haddix comprehend the magnitude of what he'd accomplished.

"I didn't even know until then I had a perfect game," he said. "I knew I had a no-hitter, but I thought they might have gotten a walk somewhere. I didn't know that nobody else had ever pitched a game like that."

Haddix, battling the flu and a sore throat on a raw, windy evening, tamed an explosive Milwaukee lineup that included right fielder Hank Aaron, third baseman Eddie Mathews and first baseman Joe Adcock, who combined for 1,603 career home runs. But through 12 innings, they were no match for Haddix.

"He had unbelievable control. He was behind in the count to only one batter in the whole game," marveled left fielder Bob Skinner. "It was just phenomenal. It was as good as you could pitch."

Q Which player broke up Haddix's no-hitter?

A Adcock, the fourth batter in the 13th inning.

Haddix lost his perfect game when leadoff batter Felix Mantilla reached on a throwing error by third baseman Don Hoak. Eddie Mathews sacrificed Mantilla to second, Hank Aaron was intentionally walked and Adcock followed with a home run.

"I meant to throw a slider down and away, but I got it up a little bit and out over the plate," Haddix recalled. "It wasn't a bad pitch, it wasn't a good pitch. It was just good enough to hit. And you have to give him credit. He didn't try to pull the ball. He just hit it over the right field fence."

But because Aaron was unaware the ball had left the park, he touched second base and then cut across the diamond toward the dugout after watching Mantilla cross home plate with the deciding run. Adcock, head down, kept circling the bases and was thus declared out for passing Aaron.

His homer became a double and what should have been a 3-0 victory officially entered the books as a 1-0 win. Not that it made much difference to the star-crossed Haddix.

Q How many National League batting titles did Honus Wagner win with the Pirates?

A Eight, a league record. Wagner captured his first crown in 1900 (.381), his last in 1911 (.334) and won four in succession starting in 1906. He finished among the NL's top five batters on four other occasions.

Roberto Clemente won four titles to rank second in Pirates history. Paul Waner (3), Dave Parker (2) and Bill Madlock (2) are the only other Bucs to claim more than one.

Wagner's total of eight NL batting crowns stood unchallenged for nearly nine decades, until San Diego's Tony Gwynn tied the record in 1997. Ty Cobb holds the major league mark with 12 titles.

DRAWING CARD

A crowd of more than 50,000 fans gathered in Pittsburgh on Oct. 4, 1908, for a Pirates game—one that wasn't even played in the city.

The Bucs opposed the Cubs in their season finale at Chicago's West Side Park, with a pennant hanging in the balance. The Pirates (98-55) led Chicago (97-55) by a half-game in the standings. With a victory, the Bucs would celebrate their first pennant since 1903.

A record crowd of 30,247 packed the park, but that congregation was dwarfed by the one in downtown Pittsburgh. Fans gathered outside the offices of several newspapers, where men with megaphones broadcast updates on the action in Chicago. The score by innings was posted on enormous bulletin boards for the benefit of those too far away to hear.

The throng was so immense that streetcar service was suspended. Traffic of all sorts came to a virtual standstill.

According to the *Pittsburg Gazette Times*, "Vehicles turned the other way until, rocking and rolling like a wave, great masses of people took undisputed possession of the streets and only permitted cars to pass when police clubbed a hole through the living mass."

The streets in the vicinity of the *Pittsburg Press* offices on Fifth Avenue were choked with humanity.

"Fifth Avenue was packed from Grant Street to Market Street and eager thousands thronged the avenue in front of the *Press* offices," noted a *Press* account. "The deepest interest was evinced in every bit of information that was forthcoming from the scene of battle."

The fans grew glum when the Cubs scored single runs off Vic Willis in the first and fifth innings for a 2-0 lead, but they exploded as Honus Wagner and Ed Abbaticchio delivered RBI hits in the sixth to tie the game.

"When two runs were hung up for Pittsburg, a roar went up from the crowd that could have been heard, like the guns at Bunker Hill, the whole world round," noted the *Gazette Times*. "But this was the only time the crowd roared. On other occasions it cried."

The Cubs answered with a run in their half of the sixth to subdue the Pittsburgh throng's enthusiasm and added single runs in the seventh and eighth. Three-Finger Brown made the lead stand up as Chicago won, 5-2.

"Never in the history of baseball," the *Gazette Times* pointed out, "was there such interest that deserves the much abused word intense, such wild hope, now bordering on confidence and again approaching despair, such frantic momentary joy—such absolute despair that was to last. The one chance that the Pirates had to win the pennant was gone."

Incidentally, 3,500 fans turned out at the Polo Grounds in New York to hear updates of the game in Chicago. The Giants, who were idle that day, were still very much alive in the race. New York (95-55) had three games yet to play with Boston, followed by a replay of a disputed tie game with the Cubs, if necessary.

The Giants swept the Braves, creating a tie for first place and setting up an Oct. 8 showdown with Chicago at the Polo Grounds. Brown outdueled Christy Mathewson in a 4-2 victory as the Cubs claimed their third consecutive pennant with a 99-55 record, one game ahead of both the Giants and Pirates—the narrowest margin among the top three teams in major league history to that point.

Q Which Yankees pitcher surrendered Bill Mazeroski's ninth-inning Game 7 home run that won the 1960 World Series for the Pirates?

A Ralph Terry, who had entered the game in the eighth inning. Maz led off the bottom of the ninth in a 9-9 game.

"The first pitch was high," Terry said. "[Catcher] John Blanchard called time and came to the mound and told me, 'This guy's a high-ball hitter. Get it down.' I got the next pitch down, but not down enough."

Mazeroski sent the delivery screaming toward the trees in Schenley Park, beyond the 406-foot mark in left field.

"I didn't try to hit a home run. I just tried to get on base," said Maz. "When I hit it I knew it was at least going to be off the wall. I was running hard, hoping to get to third, so I could score on a fly. Then the umpire gave the home run signal and I sort of went crazy."

To say the least. According to a *Newsweek* account, the normally undemonstrative Mazeroski "jumped in the air, whipped off his plastic batting helmet and began whirling his right arm, like a cheerleader gone berserk."

Mazeroski's blast was unprecedented: No previous World Series had been decided with a last-at bat home run.

Q Name the Yankees left fielder who retreated to the ivy-cloaked wall at Forbes Field and looked up helplessly as Mazeroski's homer sailed toward Schenley Park.

A Hall of Fame catcher Yogi Berra, who was often used in the outfield when not crouching behind the plate. In fact, a year later Berra appeared in more games as an outfielder (87) than he did as a catcher (15).

Q Who was the winning pitcher in Game 7?

11

A Harvey Haddix, who doused a Yankees rally in the ninth inning after Bob Friend failed to hold a 9-7 lead. He had earlier hurled the Pirates to a 5-2 victory in Game 5. Haddix admitted in later years that he took more pride in his two 1960 World Series wins than in his historic 12-inning no-hitter the year before.

Q What was located at the intersection of Bouquet and Sennott streets?

A Forbes Field. Incidentally, Bouquet was actually misspelled. It was named in honor of Swiss soldier Henry Boquet, who fought for the British in the battle of Fort Duquesne.

Q For whom was Forbes Field named?

A General John Forbes, a hero of the French and Indian War (also known as the Seven Years' War). In 1758, a British expedition led by Forbes moved on Fort Duquesne, located at the confluence of the Allegheny and Monongahela rivers, which form the Ohio. The French fled, but not before destroying the fort.

The British built their own fort on the site and named it Fort Pitt, in honor of British prime minister William Pitt. The fort was the seed that grew into the city of Pittsburgh.

Q Who selected the name?

A Pirates owner Barney Dreyfuss, who sifted through 100,000 entries in a fan contest to name the new ballpark.

Q Of what significance is Recreation Park in Pittsburgh baseball history?

A The ballpark served as the first home of the Pirates in 1887. The team played there through the 1890 season.

Recreation Park was located on a plot bounded by Grant, Allegheny and Pennsylvania avenues, with the Fort Wayne Railroad yards skirting the outfield. The site can be found today just off Allegheny Avenue, several blocks north of Three Rivers Stadium. However, there's no evidence that a ballpark was once located on the site.

Q Where did the Pirates play after that?

A Exposition Park, which stood several hundred feet upriver from Three Rivers. In fact, the position of home plate, the pitching rubber and the bases are painted onto the surface of a parking lot that today serves the stadium.

Actually, there were two previous Exposition Parks, also located on the North Side, that were utilized by Pittsburgh's American Association and Union Association teams from 1882 to 1884. The Pirates played their last game at Exposition Park III on June 29, 1909, the day before Forbes Field's grand opening.

Q All-around standout Honus Wagner, left fielder Fred Clarke, third baseman Tommy Leach, pitcher Deacon Phillippe and second baseman Claude Ritchey—the core of the Pirates' pennant teams of 1901-03—were among the 14 players obtained by Pittsburgh from another franchise when the National League pared its membership from 12 teams to eight following the 1899 season. In what city had they played?

A Louisville. The Colonels, who were admitted to the American Association in 1885, joined the National League in 1892 following the demise of the AA. Louisville owner Barney Dreyfuss acquired a half interest in the Pirates, became the club's owner and brought the bulk of his old team to Pittsburgh, immediately transforming the Bucs into pennant contenders.

SPRING IN THE SOUTH

T he Pirates and Cleveland Spiders launched a trend on April 2, 1891, simply by clashing in an exhibition game at St. Augustine, Fla. It was the first spring training contest ever played in Florida between major league teams.

The clubs were originally scheduled to square off on March 28, but circumstances beyond the Bucs' control canceled the game. According to the *Pittsburg Post*, the team "met with a railroad accident, which delayed its arrival 10 hours and prevented the game with the Clevelands this afternoon."

Cy Young hurled the Spiders to an 8-6 victory on April 2 before a crowd of 600 at Ponce de Leon Park. First baseman Jake Beckley paced the Pittsburgh assault with three hits.

"The Pittsburgers got on to the hang of the game in fine shape, and although somewhat stiff, made things lively and could afford to give their opponents the first of the three successive games to be played," noted the Post. "The large audience was made up of lovers of base ball, including many ladies."

The Pirates won the second game of the series the next day, 5-3. Cleveland took the rubber match on April 4 by a score of 6-3.

Q Which Pirates outfielder caused Brooklyn fans to howl with laughter during a 1918 game, simply by raising his cap?

A Casey Stengel, who had spotted an injured sparrow hopping along the base of the right field wall at Ebbets Field. Stengel carefully picked up the bird and placed it under his cap temporarily for safe-keeping.

The absent-minded Casey had forgotten about his feathered captive as he stepped to the plate for the first time an inning later. When Stengel received a warm round of applause from the fans—he had played for Brooklyn the six previous seasons—he doffed his cap in appreciation and the sparrow flew out. The crowd roared with laughter.

Q Who threw the first no-hitter in Pirates history?

A Rookie Nicholas Maddox, who victimized the Brooklyn Superbas— later the Dodgers—by a 2-1 score on Sept. 20, 1907, before a gathering of 2,380 at Exposition Park.

"Not even the semblance of a hit was made by the Brooklyns," crowed the *Pittsburgh Gazette Times*. "Now, this is saying much, as there are always some people who will split a hair, but no hairsplitting could be done yesterday, because not a ghost of a hit was visible."

The Superbas scored an unearned run in the fourth inning on two errors, but the Pirates tied the game in the fifth. Pittsburgh then grabbed the lead for good in the seventh when Honus Wagner walked, advanced to third on a wild throw and raced home when George Gibson bounced into a force at second.

Maddox wrapped up his third no-hitter of the season—he tossed two with Wheeling of the Central League—when Wagner rode to his rescue.

"The only time the Brooklyns had a chance for a bingle was in the ninth, when [Emil] Batch hit a slow grounder to Wagner," noted a *Pittsburgh Leader* account. "The mighty shortstop made a quick play, however, and nabbed his man at first, thereby ending the game."

Sixty-nine years passed before another Pirates pitcher threw a no-hitter in Pittsburgh. Like Maddox, John Candelaria tamed the Dodgers. Despite an aching back, Candelaria handcuffed Los Angeles 2-0 at Three Rivers Stadium on Aug. 9, 1976.

Q Harold Arlin holds a special place in Pirates—and major league—history, yet he never wore a uniform. What is his claim to fame?

A Arlin was behind the microphone at Forbes Field on Aug. 5, 1921, broadcasting the Bucs' 8-5 win over the Phillies on KDKA—the first radio coverage of a major league game. Yet the 26-year-old studio announcer did not consider himself a pioneer.

"Our broadcast—back then, at least—wasn't that big a deal," he recalled years later. "Our guys at KDKA didn't even think that baseball would last on radio. I did it sort of as a one-shot project."

One Arlin who *did* wear a major league uniform was Harold's grandson, Steve, who pitched for San Diego and Cleveland (1969-74).

Q At what age did Honus Wagner—generally acknowledged as the greatest shortstop in baseball history—first play the position in the major leagues?

A 27. Wagner had appeared in the outfield, at second base, third base and first base and even pitched before trying shortstop in 1901, his fifth season in the majors. It wasn't until 1903 that he was installed as the Pirates' regular shortstop. Long-time New York Giants manager John McGraw once said of Wagner, "He was the nearest thing to a perfect player, no matter where his manager chose to play him."

Q Which Pirate captured a league home run crown without once hitting a ball over the fence?

A "Wee" Tommy Leach, a 5-6½, 150-pound third baseman for the National League champions of 1902.

He hit six homers that season, every one of them an inside-the-park blow. That represents the lowest total by a league leader in modern major league history.

Leach played half his games at Exposition Park, where the absurd dimensions—400 feet down the lines and 450 to center—discouraged any attempts to power balls beyond the fences.

"I wasn't a home run hitter like you see today," Leach said years later. "The fields were big then, and if you hit a ball between the outfielders and were fast enough, you had a home run."

Exposition Park was so ludicrously large that on July 22, 1908, Brooklyn's Tim Jordan—that year's major league home run leader with 12—drew oohs and aahs by slugging the first over-the-fence homer in Pittsburgh in *nine* years.

Q Name the Pirates pitcher who, at the age of 43, gained the distinction of being the oldest rookie in big league history.

A Diomedes Olivo, who debuted with the Bucs on Sept. 5, 1960, at the tender age of 41. Because he worked only nine and two-thirds innings that season, Olivo was still technically a rookie when he returned to the majors two years later.

The Dominican reliever went 5-1 for the 1962 Pirates before wrapping up his career with the Cardinals in 1963. Brother Chi-Chi was also a late bloomer, arriving in the majors with the Braves in 1961 at the age of 33.

Only former Negro Leagues standout Satchel Paige (42 years, two days) was older than Diomedes Olivo when he debuted in the majors. Fact is, Paige might have actually been older than 42 when he made his first appearance for the Indians on July 9, 1948.

When the question of age was raised, Paige invariably pleaded ignorance, explaining that a goat ate his birth certificate back home in Mobile, Ala. He gave his birth year as 1906, although doubts lingered about the validity of that claim.

Especially when Ted "Double Duty" Radcliffe, Paige's teammate with the Pittsburgh Crawfords in 1932 and a fellow Mobile native, insisted he was younger than Paige. Radcliffe was born in 1902.

Q Oct. 17, 1971, was a special day for this Pirate—he celebrated a world championship in the afternoon and his wedding that night. Name him.

A Pitcher Bruce Kison, who married Anna Marie Orlando only hours after Pittsburgh defeated the Orioles 2-1 at Baltimore's Municipal Stadium in Game 7 of the World Series.

A helicopter ferried Kison and best man Bob Moose from the stadium to the airport, where a private jet was waiting to whisk them to Pittsburgh for the ceremony at Churchill Valley Country Club. Kison was only 40 minutes late for the scheduled 7 p.m. nuptials.

QThe losingest team in modern Pirates history finished 22½ games behind Boston—*seventh-place* Boston—in the eight-team National League. In what year did the hapless Bucs crawl home with a 42-112 record?

A1952. Only six teams in major league history have lost more games.

Those Pirates were so anemic that wise-cracking catcher Joe Garagiola finished second on the team in batting (.273) and third in home runs (8) and RBIs (54). They accomplished a dubious trifecta by ranking dead last in batting, pitching and fielding.

"It was the most courageous team in baseball," Garagiola said. "We had 154 games scheduled and we showed up for every one."

QThe worst team in Pirates history was not the 1952 club—the 1890 Bucs were even more pathetic. How many games did they win?

A23. The Pirates limped home with a 23-113 record and lost a franchise-record 23 consecutive games in one stretch. Pittsburgh was thin in talent that year because four starters (including center fielder-manager Ned Hanlon) and the team's three best pitchers defected to the rival Players League.

DISAPPEARING ACT

Pirates pitcher Pascual Perez and Dodgers outfielder Reggie Smith were the principals in one of the most unusual altercations in baseball history. That's because it took place not on the diamond, but under the stands.

Smith was riding Perez from the bench for throwing too close to the Los Angeles batters (in fact, Bill Russell and Dusty Baker were hit by pitches in the sixth inning) during the teams' Aug. 25, 1981, game at Three Rivers Stadium. Perez shouted back and Smith responded by suggesting they "meet" under the stands at the close of the inning.

The Pirates, several of whom were brandishing bats, followed Perez from the dugout down a runway leading to a common hallway, where Smith and the Dodgers soon arrived. The umpires then went in search of the teams. The 16,770 fans were left to gaze at a deserted diamond and wonder what happened. The teams engaged in some pushing and shoving, but no blows were exchanged and no one was ejected.

"It was just like a fight out on the field," said Russell. "Nobody swings—just a lot of screaming and yelling."

Los Angeles won the game in 11 innings by a 9-7 score.

Q Which Pirate appeared on *The Ed Sullivan Show* in New York?

A First baseman Dale Long, who was introduced to the crowd and a national television audience on May 27, 1956, in honor of his unprecedented feat of slugging home runs in seven consecutive games.

That day's doubleheader in Philadelphia had been rained out, so Long agreed to appear on the popular Sunday night variety show. Singer Kate Smith headed the bill.

Long bettered his record the following night at Forbes Field by smashing No. 8.

Q Which pitcher did Long victimize?

A Brooklyn's Carl Erskine, who had thrown a no-hitter 16 days before.

Q Which pitcher halted Long's streak?

A Brooklyn's Don Newcombe, the Cy Young award winner and National League MVP that season on the strength of a 27-7 record. Long went 0-for-4 the afternoon of May 29 after getting to bed late following the previous night's game and then rising early to appear on the *Today* show, hosted by Dave Garroway, via a Pittsburgh television studio.

"The newspaper fellows afterward said that Newcombe overpowered me, but the fact is I was tired," said Long on the 30th anniversary of his feat. "I was so beat I couldn't get my bat around. You can't do that and face Newcombe and expect to hit a homer."

Long did smash a 430-foot drive, but center fielder Duke Snider flagged it down in deep right center.

Two players have since matched Long's record: Don Mattingly of the Yankees (1987) and Seattle's Ken Griffey Jr. (1993).

Q Which Pirates pitcher "threw" himself in front of the team bus during Long's hot streak?

A Nellie King, who posted two of his seven career victories during his teammate's long-ball binge. The bus incident occurred in Philadelphia, after Long's home run streak had reached a record-tying six games.

"Because of all the interest, the Philly writers were doing a lot of interviews with Dale. The players were waiting on the bus," King recalled. "Finally, a couple of them started shouting, 'C'mon, let's go, he can get a cab.' "

King stood up and barked, "we're not leaving till he gets here." He then stepped outside and stretched out defiantly in front of the bus. It didn't budge until Long was aboard.

Q Of what significance is the Huntingdon Avenue Baseball Grounds in Pirates—and major league—a history?

A The ballpark in downtown Boston was the site of the first World Series game, played between the Pirates and Pilgrims on Oct. 1, 1903.

Q Horace Phillips was the first individual in Pirates history to do what?

A Manage the club. The 33-year-old Phillips, who never played at the major league level, led the 1887 Bucs to a 55-69 record, good for sixth place in the eight-team National League.

"Hustling Horace" was no stranger to Pittsburgh: He accepted the managerial reins of the city's foundering American Association team late in the 1884 season, then led the Alleghenys to third- and second-place finishes in 1885 and 1886, respectively.

Phillips' Pirates career ended halfway through the 1889 season when he suffered a nervous breakdown and took a leave of absence. Phillips was confined to a mental institution, from which he never emerged.

Q In what year did the Pirates sport two defending major league home run champions in their lineup?

A 1947. Left fielder Ralph Kiner had slugged 23 homers as a rookie the year before to edge out Johnny Mize of the Giants (22) for the National League crown. First baseman Hank Greenberg, a boyhood idol of Kiner's, had hit 44 homers for Detroit in 1946 to claim the American League title.

The Tigers, unwilling to cough up Greenberg's substantial salary for another year, sold him to the Bucs for $75,000. Kiner and Greenberg became roommates, good friends and, ultimately, fellow members of baseball's Hall of Fame.

Q Who was the Pirates' first 20-game winner?

A Hall of Famer James "Pud" Galvin, who fashioned a 28-21 record in 1887, the Bucs' inaugural season. Galvin won 20 or more games 10 times during his illustrious career.

Q How many times have the Pirates played host to the major league All-Star game?

A Four, with the National League emerging victorious on each occasion: 7-1 in 1944, 5-4 in 1959, 7-2 in 1974 and 8-7 in 1994.

SLEEPING BEAUTY

The only loss of his Pirates career apparently drove Joe Sullivan to drink. And to fall asleep in a place where, quite possibly, no one ever had before.

Brooklyn battered the 30-year-old veteran in a 9-0 loss at Ebbets Field on Aug. 19, 1941. Sullivan probably felt even worse the next day—if he felt anything at all. He showed up drunk and hid out from his manager and coaches in the bullpen before curling up inside a tarp and falling fast asleep.

Sullivan, obtained from the Braves on waivers a month before, was suspended 30 days and fined $200 for what one newspaper account delicately termed "breaking training."

His troubles began a day earlier when the Dodgers shelled him for seven runs in two-thirds of an inning. Sullivan sought solace with a bottle.

"He arrived at Ebbets Field in a none too good condition, dressed hurriedly and went out on the field before manager Frankie Frisch or his coaches saw him," wrote Les Biederman in the *Pittsburgh Press*. "During the game he crawled inside one of the huge shells used for the tarpaulins and slept there. When Frisch located him, the fine and suspension followed. Frisch, ever the gentleman, didn't awaken him until the heart-breaking game was over."

Biederman characterized the game thusly because the Bucs committed five errors en route to a 7-6 loss. Tongue planted firmly in cheek, he wrote, "The fact that Sullivan slept through yesterday's fiasco indicates he isn't as dumb as some persons think."

Ironically, the defeat that prompted Sullivan to fall off the wagon was his only setback with the Pirates. Otherwise he was 4-0 during his brief stay with the Bucs.

Q Who were "Big Poison" and "Little Poison"?

A The Waner brothers, Paul and Lloyd. The Waners were a menace to opposing pitchers: Paul batted .333 for his career and little brother Lloyd posted a .316 average. Between them, they pounded out 5,611 hits, more than any other brother act in big league history.

Noted the Cubs' Charlie Grimm, who played and managed against the Waners, "Their only weakness is they can't hit balls rolled under the plate."

Q The brother acts who rank second, third and fourth behind the Waners as far as career hits each featured one sibling who played for the Pirates. Name them.

A The Alous—Felipe (2,101), Matty (1,777) and Jesus (1,216)—totaled 5,094 hits between 1958 and 1979 to place second on the all-time list. The DiMaggios—Joe (2,214), Dom (1,680) and Vince (959)—rank third with 4,853 hits and the five Delahantys—Ed (2,597), Jim (1,159), Frank (223), Joe (222) and Tom (16)—stand fourth with 4,217.

Matty Alou (1966-70), Vince DiMaggio (1940-44) and Tom Delahanty (1896) all played with Pittsburgh.

Q The Pirates have spent 31 spring trainings in Bradenton, Fla., more than anywhere else. Which destination ranks second?

A Hot Springs, Ark. (18 years). The Bucs trained there from 1901 through 1914 and again from 1920 through 1923. Fort Myers, Fla. (14) and San Bernardino, Calif., (12) were also popular spring sites. The Pirates have trained in Bradenton every year since 1969.

Q The Bucs once spent spring training in another country. Which one?

A Cuba. The Pirates established their camp at Club Nautico de Marianao—a yacht club just outside Havana—in 1953, although they were less than enthused about the experience. A six-week sojourn seemed like a six-year sentence to the players, who nearly launched their own Cuban revolution over the appalling conditions.

In fact, the team was so eager to break camp on April 4 that, according to a *Pittsburgh Post-Gazette* account, a bus scheduled to leave for the airport at 6:30 a.m. was loaded and ready to go at 6:10.

"I don't remember that, but it wouldn't surprise me," said catcher Joe Garagiola. "It wouldn't surprise me if it said the bus was loaded at 6:10 the day *before*. Anxious to get out of there? I should say we were."

The downtrodden Bucs, coming off a 42-112 season, were no strangers to misery. But even *their* capacity for suffering was tested by dreadful food, third-rate accommodations, withering heat, a chewed-up diamond and uninvited guests—bullfrogs and mosquitoes—that invaded their sleeping quarters.

"If it were up to the members of the Pittsburgh Pirates to decide, they would vote to dump this 'Paris of the Western World,' as it is advertised, into the nearby water surrounding this ancient isle," wrote Al Abrams in the *Post-Gazette*. "In all my travels to baseball training camps, I have never found a more disgruntled group of players. They are openly hostile about their living accommodations, the food they have to eat and innumerable other minor details. 'It's no way to treat even a last-place ball club,' moaned one veteran."

Mealtimes were especially grim. The fare was so unpalatable that third baseman Pete Castiglione relied on peanut butter and jelly just to get by. Abrams reported an encounter with a piece a meat "tougher than Joe Garagiola's glove." And about as flavorful.

"The food was brutal," Garagiola recalled. "When we came back [to the States], I remember someone saying, 'Hey, you guys look like you're in great shape.' Well, we were thin. We hadn't eaten down there. It was like permanent Lent."

The Pirates never went back to Cuba. In fact, they're the last major league team to set up a spring training camp outside the United States.

Q Where did the Pirates establish their spring training base during World War II?

A Muncie, Ind. Because of government-imposed travel restrictions, the 16 big league clubs were confined to training sites north of the Ohio and Potomac rivers and east of the Mississippi for the 1943, 1944 and 1945 seasons.

Indiana, rather than Florida, served as the center of the spring training universe during the war years. Five teams besides Pittsburgh set up camps there—the Reds, Indians, Tigers, Cubs and White Sox.

Warming up took on a whole new meaning at the northern sites, where players were as apt to toss snowballs as baseballs during workouts.

They bundled up like polar explorers and weathered a stew of hardships cooked up by Mother Nature.

"It was so much different than a regular spring training," recalled outfielder Al Gionfriddo.

How different? The Pirates would dash into the locker room following workouts, where two roaring log fires awaited them. Cold wasn't their only meteorological adversary. Manager Frankie Frisch occasionally had to dispatch a broom brigade to McCulloch Park following an overnight snowfall so practice could proceed as planned.

"I remember once we had to shovel the snow off," recalled pitcher Xavier Rescigno. "It was a high school diamond, so it wasn't in good shape to begin with. We did the groundskeeping ourselves."

No wonder the Pirates welcomed a return to their pre-war training base in San Bernardino, Calif., in 1946.

Q Who is sometimes referred to as "The Father of the World Series"?

A Barney Dreyfuss, long-time owner of the Pirates. Dreyfuss challenged Henry Killilea, his counterpart with the American League champion Boston Pilgrims, to a postseason playoff in 1903 to determine which was the better team. The World Series was thus born.

Q The Pirates have retired the numbers of eight players and managers, the last seven being Honus Wagner (33 in 1956), Pie Traynor (20 in 1972), Roberto Clemente (21 in 1973), Danny Murtaugh (40 in 1977), Willie Stargell (8 in 1982), Bill Mazeroski (9 in 1987) and Ralph Kiner (4 in 1987). Name the first.

A Billy Meyer, who managed the Bucs from 1948 to 1952. Meyer had his number (1) retired in 1954. His record, for the record, was nothing to brag about: 317-452.

Q What was unusual about Wagner's retired number?

A He never wore it as a player. Wagner's career ended in 1917, 12 years before the Yankees became the first major league club to regularly wear numerals, home and away. Wagner did wear No. 33 as a long-time Pirates coach (1933-51).

Q The colorful Bob Prince spent 28 years as a Pirates broadcaster, the longest tenure in team history. Who ranks second?

A Lanny Frattare, who celebrated his 24th season with the Bucs in 1999. Rosey Rowswell ranks third in terms of service with 19 years (1936-54).

THE GOOSE-EGG GANG

O ne of the most phenomenal exhibitions of sustained mound mastery in major league history occurred during the 1903 season, when the Pirates' pitching staff strung together goose-eggs in record numbers. Pittsburgh hurlers shut out the opposition for 56 consecutive innings to set a big league standard that hasn't been equaled.

The Bucs' whitewash wizardry began on June 1 and ended June 9, with a major league-record six consecutive shutouts in between. Sam Leever and Deacon Phillippe hurled two shutouts apiece during the streak, which was treated as something of a mystery by one Pittsburgh newspaper.

"Trouble has arisen over the disappearance of the home plate at Expo Park," noted the *Press*. "For a number of days, the players of visiting clubs have been searching for the missing plate, but not one of them has been able to get a glimpse of it."

Until June 9, that is, when Philadelphia's Roy Thomas scored on a sacrifice fly by John Titus off rookie pitcher Kaiser Wilhelm. The Phillies rushed from the dugout in celebration, as if they'd just won a pennant. A headline in the next day's *Press* read, "Home plate at Expo Park is found."

Shutouts had become so commonplace, noted the *Press*, that "the question asked during the games these days is not 'Will Pittsburg win?' but 'Will the other side score?' "

Q What incredible streak did Charlie Neal of the Dodgers end on Sept. 11, 1959, with a game-winning single against the Bucs?

A Reliever Elroy Face's run of 22 consecutive victories without a loss, only two shy of the big league standard set by Giants great Carl Hubbell over the 1936 and 1937 seasons. Face was seemingly invincible, boasting a 17-0 record.

But Neal's RBI single off Face through a drawn-in infield in the bottom of the ninth gave the Dodgers a 5-4 win and halted a streak that stretched back to May of 1958, a span of 98 appearances.

Said Face afterwards, "Don Drysdale lost two games one day at Forbes Field, so I guess I'm entitled to lose one game in a year and a half."

Q What was Face's record that season?

A 18-1, good for a .947 winning percentage, the best in big league history (minimum of 15 decisions). The 18 victories also represents a single-season record for relievers.

Q Face holds the Pirates record for consecutive wins in a season, with 17 in 1959. What's the team standard for consecutive victories by a starting pitcher?

A 13, a record shared by Frank Killen (1893), Deacon Phillippe (1910) and Dock Ellis (1971).

Q Youthful California newspaper heir Kevin McClatchy was named the Pirates' chief executive officer and managing general partner on Feb. 14, 1996. How many previous owners has the club had this century?

A Only four: Barney Dreyfuss (1900-32), Dreyfuss' son-in-law Bill Benswanger (1932-46), John Galbreath (1946-85) and Pittsburgh Associates (1985-96), a consortium of investors.

Q Who threw out the ceremonial first ball when the Pirates hosted the 1959 All-Star game at Forbes Field?

A Vice President Richard Nixon, who was accompanied to the game by his 13-year-old daughter, Tricia.

Q What nationally known comedy trio upstaged Nixon that afternoon?

A The Three Stooges, who were especially popular in Pittsburgh. The madcap threesome—then consisting of Moe, Larry and Curly—clowned around with broadcaster Dizzy Dean at home plate before the game, stealing the spotlight from Nixon.

The Stooges regularly appeared live on *Paul Shannon's Adventure Time*, a children's program that originated at the WTAE-TV studios in Pittsburgh.

Q This son of a famous actor-comedian was deadly serious about turning the lowly Pirates into winners when he was hired as the team's general manager in 1956. Four years later—thanks in part to his shrewd trades— the Bucs reigned as world champions. Name him.

A Joe L. Brown, the son of Joe E. Brown, a star of vaudeville and burlesque who later appeared on Broadway and in films, where he was renowned for his elastic face and slapstick style. Brown made his movie debut in 1928 in *Crooks Can't Win*; one of his final films was *It's a Mad, Mad, Mad, Mad World* in 1963. He also appeared in *Some Like it Hot* (1959) with Marilyn Monroe. Brown played semipro baseball before becoming a full-time entertainer.

His son served as the Pirates' GM through the 1976 season and returned briefly in 1985. Brown built the foundation for the championship team of 1960, acquiring Bill Virdon, Don Hoak, Wilmer Mizell, Rocky Nelson, Harvey Haddix and Smoky Burgess in deals and promoting Danny Murtaugh from coach to manager in 1957.

The Pirates won two world titles, two league championships and five division crowns in Brown's 22 seasons with the club.

Q Only 11 players in major league history have pulled off unassisted triple plays. Which Pirate is a member of this exclusive club?

A Shortstop Glenn Wright, who turned the trick at Forbes Field on May 7, 1925, against the Cardinals. Wright snared Jim Bottomley's line drive, stepped on second to retire Jimmy Cooney and then tagged Rogers Hornsby coming down from first to end the game.

Cooney gained a measure of revenge two years later at Forbes Field, joining the club at the Pirates' expense. He was then a member of the Cubs. Cooney is the only player in major league history to be involved in two unassisted triple plays.

Q Which Pirate properly rounds out this list of players—Ty Cobb, Walter Johnson, Christy Mathewson and Babe Ruth?

A Honus Wagner. Those five players were elected as charter members of baseball's Hall of Fame in 1936.

THE DEATH OF A HERO

On Dec. 31, 1972, Roberto Clemente climbed aboard a dangerously overloaded DC-7 cargo plane packed with relief supplies destined for victims of a Nicaraguan earthquake.

It wasn't enough that Clemente headed Puerto Rico's relief committee, collecting food, clothing and medicine for the thousands of Nicaraguans left homeless by the Dec. 23 disaster. The Pirates right fielder felt compelled to accompany the flight from San Juan to Nicaragua's capital city of Managua.

That fateful decision cost Clemente his life.

The plane plunged into the Atlantic Ocean moments after takeoff, killing all five aboard. Puerto Rico, Pittsburgh and all of baseball mourned Clemente's passing at the age of 38.

"Words seem futile in the face of this tragedy, nor can they possibly do justice to this unique man," said commissioner Bowie Kuhn. "Somehow, Roberto transcended superstardom. His marvelous playing skills rank him among the truly elite. And what a wonderfully good man he was, always concerned about others."

That concern prompted Clemente to leave his family on New Year's Eve and fly to Nicaragua. He was appalled to learn that some earlier shipments had fallen into the hands of profiteers. Clemente hoped his presence—he was idolized throughout the Caribbean and Central America—would discourage looters. But the plane was airborne for only a few minutes before plummeting into the sea.

Clemente left a widow, Vera, and three young sons: Roberto, Luis and Enrique. It was in keeping with his selfless nature that he died extending a helping hand to those less fortunate. Clemente was eulogized as a great ballplayer, but as an even greater humanitarian.

"If you have to die, how better could your death be exemplified than by dying on a mission of mercy?" said Pirates owner John Galbreath. "It was so typical of the man."

Q Who succeeded Clemente as the Pirates' starting right fielder the following season?

A His close friend, Manny Sanguillen, a catcher who had previously played only two major league games in the outfield. However, the experiment was soon abandoned. Rookie Richie Zisk inherited Clemente's old position in June, when Sanguillen moved back behind the plate for good.

Q The Pirates won their first World Series in 1909 due in large measure to which rookie pitcher?

A Charles Adams. Better known as Babe, he tamed the Tigers while more experienced teammates faltered. Adams won and completed all three of his starts, permitting only four earned runs and 18 hits.

Meanwhile, Howie Camnitz, Vic Willis and Al Leifield—who combined for 66 victories during the season—failed to win a game. Their aggregate earned run average was 6.63, well above Adams' 1.33.

Q Before Ralph Kiner brought his booming bat to Pittsburgh, what was the team record for home runs in a season?

A 23, set in 1938 by rookie left fielder Johnny Rizzo. Eight years later another rookie left fielder—Kiner—matched that modest standard before obliterating it the following season with 51 home runs.

Q What was incredible about Kiner's 51-homer season in 1947?

A He had cracked only three by the end of May and was nearly demoted to the minors. Manager Billy Herman wanted to farm out the struggling Kiner, but teammate Hank Greenberg prevailed upon club president Frank McKinney and general manager Roy Hamey to exercise patience.

Greenberg volunteered to act as a mentor to the 24-year-old slugger. His tutelage helped Kiner pull out of his slump and catch fire. He clouted 48 home runs over the last four months of the season, including a major league-record eight in one four-game stretch.

"Hank put me in a better position in the batter's box, which enabled me to pull outside pitches," said Kiner, a New York Mets broadcaster since 1962. "He changed my stance and my whole approach to hitting, getting me to not swing at bad pitches."

Q The 51 home runs Kiner clubbed in 1947 do not represent the franchise record. How many did Kiner hit two years later?

A 54. Only three National Leaguers have hit more: Mark McGwire of the Cardinals (70 in 1998) and Sammy Sosa (66 in 1998) and Hack Wilson of the Cubs (56 in 1930). Kiner slugged 9.84 homers per 100 at bats in 1949, which ranks him third in NL history behind only McGwire (13.75) and Sosa (10.26), whose riveting home run duel went down to the final day of the 1998 season.

What's more, Kiner won the home run crown by 18 (Stan Musial finished second with 36), a margin unsurpassed by any National Leaguer since. Only three players in major league history—Ruth (six times), Mickey Mantle (1956) and Cy Williams of the 1923 Phillies—have claimed titles by wider margins.

Q Where does Kiner rank on the career home run ratio list?

A Third, with an average of 7.09 homers per 100 at bats. Only Mark McGwire (8.91) and Babe Ruth (8.50) are above him. Kiner led the National League in home run ratio in each of his seven full seasons in Pittsburgh (1946-52).

Q Kiner concluded his Pirates career in 1953 with 301 home runs, at that time a club record. Who held it before he arrived in Pittsburgh?

A Paul Waner, with 109 between 1926 and 1940. Kiner eclipsed that total before his third season with the Bucs had run its course.

Q This second baseman was selected as the MVP of the 1960 World Series. Name him.

A Bill Mazeroski? No, MVP honors went to Bobby Richardson, the Yankees' No. 8 hitter and, in the words of one reporter, "The mouse that roared."

Richardson batted .367 and set a Series record with 12 runs batted in, an unprecedented six of them in Game 3. Both marks still stand.

Ironically, Richardson had knocked home only 26 runs in 150 regular-season games. Following his six-RBI outburst against the Bucs, a teammate told Richardson, "Your name looks funny beside a record." He was certainly an unlikely candidate to generate offensive fireworks: Casey Stengel didn't hesitate to bat him ninth on occasion in previous years.

Richardson is the only Series MVP to play for the losing team.

Q Name the successor to each of these Pirates managers: Bobby Bragan, Harry Walker, Larry Shepard and Bill Virdon.

A The answer in all four instances is Danny Murtaugh, who holds the National League record for most managerial stints with one club. Billy Martin of the Yankees, a frequent rider on George Steinbrenner's managerial merry-go-round, owns the major league mark: five.

"Managing a ball club," Murtaugh said, "is like getting malaria—once you've been bitten by the bug, it's difficult to get it out of your bloodstream."

He replaced Bragan during the 1957 season, Walker during the 1967 season, Shepard following the 1969 season (coach Alex Grammas had served as interim manager for five games at the tail end of the year) and Virdon during the 1973 season.

Murtaugh retired for good in 1976, the last of his 15 seasons managing the club. Health problems—he had suffered two heart attacks and was plagued by a variety of other ailments—forced him to the sidelines.

"That was a major reason," said Murtaugh, explaining his decision to retire at the age of 58. "I've been ill a few times this year when few people realized it. I think it's time for a younger man to take over."

Murtaugh, a craggy-faced, teetotaling Irishman whose post-game drink of choice was milk, led the Pirates to 1,115 victories, two world championships and four division crowns.

"In my younger years, I don't think I spent enough time with my children," he said in his farewell announcement. "I'm retiring to kind of make it up with my grandchildren."

Sadly, Murtaugh was denied that opportunity. He suffered a stroke on Nov. 30, lapsed into a coma and died on Dec. 2—less than two months after his final game at the helm.

A Deadly Drink

Tom O'Brien, who appeared in 209 games as a Pirates first baseman and outfielder during the seasons of 1898 and 1900, died at the age of 27—from drinking seawater.

In the fall of 1900, O'Brien joined a group of National Leaguers recruited mostly from the New York and Brooklyn teams—he had started in left field for the Giants in 1899—en route to Cuba for an exhibition series.

As the ship steamed from New York harbor, O'Brien was told that drinking seawater would, after an initial bit of discomfort, prevent seasickness. He and Giants second baseman Kid Gleason followed this advice, but O'Brien drank so much his internal organs were affected. Unable to play, he returned to New York, where a doctor informed him his heart, stomach and kidneys were seriously weakened.

O'Brien headed to Arizona in hopes of regaining his health, but he never recovered. He died in Phoenix on Feb. 4, 1901.

Q Besides seven-time champ Ralph Kiner, how many Pirates have won home run crowns?

A Only two—Tommy Leach in 1902 and Willie Stargell in 1971 and 1973. Discounting expansion franchises, no National League team has produced fewer different home run champions.

This decided dearth of long-ball leaders stems, in great measure, from the distant outfield walls at Exposition Park and, later, Forbes Field. Long-time owner Barney Dreyfuss, who oversaw the design of Forbes Field, reportedly detested cheap home runs and vowed there would be none at the new ballpark.

"How can a fellow hit home runs in Pittsburgh?" first baseman Dick Stuart once asked. "It's a five-buck cab fare to the closest fence."

One writer described Forbes Field's vast expanses as only "slightly smaller than the Gobi Desert."

Q Which Pirates manager led his team to the most league titles?

A Fred Clarke, who guided Pittsburgh to National League pennants in 1901, 1902, 1903 and 1909 and to the world championship in 1909. Clarke also managed the Pirates longer than anyone else—16 seasons—and won more games (1,422).

Q Name the last Pirate to reach the 200-hit milestone.

A Dave Parker, who banged out a league-leading 215 hits back in 1977, the season he captured the first of his two batting titles. For the record, 49 different major leaguers have topped 200 hits on 81 occasions since then, through the 1998 season.

Parker's total is the second-highest by a Pirate over the last 70 seasons, trailing only Matty Alou's NL-leading 231 hits in 1966. Paul Waner set the franchise record in 1927 with 237, tied for 17th-best on the all-time single-season list. Waner posted 200 or more hits on eight occasions, a total exceeded by only two players: Pete Rose (10) and Ty Cobb (9).

Q Name the first Pirate to start in an All-Star game.

A Hall of Famer Pie Traynor, who started at third base in 1934. Traynor was then in his 15th major league season.

Q Who was the first Pirate to hit safely in an All-Star game?

A Traynor again. He rapped a pinch double off the Athletics' Lefty Grove in the inaugural game at Chicago's Comiskey Park in 1933.

Q Which member of the Chicago Cubs hit the so-called Homer in the Gloamin' that crushed the Pirates' pennant hopes in 1938?

A Catcher-manager Gabby Hartnett, whose two-out, two-strike, ninth-inning home run in the fading light at Wrigley Field gave the Cubs a dramatic 6-5 victory on Sept. 28, enabling them to leapfrog Pittsburgh into first place. The ball was barely visible as it left the park.

Chicago, which trailed the Pirates by a game and a half entering the crucial three-game series, swept Pittsburgh and never looked back. The Bucs finished in second place, two games behind the Cubs.

"I guess technically we still could have won the pennant," recalled Paul Waner, who played right field in that pivotal game. "There were still a couple days left to the season. But that home run took all the fight out of us. It broke our hearts."

Q Which pitcher did Hartnett victimize?

A Mace Brown, the Pirates' leading winner that season with a 15-9 record. Unfortunately, his name will be forever linked with a demoralizing defeat.

"It kept me awake nights, thinking," Brown said during a Pirates' Old-Timers game nearly half a century later. "Of course, I'm not the only one it's happened to. But when I kick off . . . I always said my name will be in the papers twice—when I die and when Hartnett dies. I know they'll mention me."

Q This Hall of Famer spent six years with the Pirates as a catcher and also managed the team for parts of three seasons. But he's most identified with another Pennsylvania team, which he served for half a century. Name him.

A Connie Mack, who directed the Philadelphia Athletics from 1901 to 1950, by far the longest managerial reign in major league history.

Mack caught with the Bucs from 1891 to 1896 and managed the club from 1894 to 1896.

Q Which player broke the Pirates' color barrier?

A Curt Roberts, a 24-year-old rookie who reached the majors in 1954 and was immediately installed as the Bucs' starting second baseman. The team's general manager then was Branch Rickey, who had challenged baseball's exclusionary policy seven years before as the Brooklyn Dodgers' GM by bringing Jackie Robinson to the big leagues.

"Roberts first Negro to make Pirates," trumpeted a *Pittsburgh Post-Gazette* headline heralding his arrival. He delivered a triple in three at bats as the Bucs rolled to a 4-2 victory over Philadelphia in the April 13 season opener at Forbes Field.

Roberts' coming-out party, unlike Robinson's in 1947, generated little in the way of fanfare—or hate mail. To the media, to the spectators, to the Pirates themselves, the complexion of the newcomer was immaterial.

"It really wasn't that much of an issue," recalled pitcher Nellie King, who also joined the team in 1954. "We didn't think of him as a black guy. He was just a player. He could be a pain in the ass at times and a real nice kid at times, just like anyone else."

Roberts was born in Pineland, Texas. His family moved to California—as Robinson's did, from Georgia—where he earned four letters in baseball at McClymonds High School in Oakland. McClymonds, incidentally, produced two other notable sports pioneers: basketball Hall of Famer Bill Russell, the NBA's first black head coach, and Hall of Fame outfielder Frank Robinson, the majors' first black manager.

Unfortunately, Roberts never approached the professional achievements of Russell or either Robinson. He appeared in only 37 major league games after his breakthrough 1954 season and batted .223 lifetime with one home run. His future with the Pirates was effectively sealed in July of 1956 when the Bucs summoned a 19-year-old whiz kid from their Hollywood farm club named William Stanley Mazeroski. The man who made history *was* history.

It was somehow fitting that Roberts' last year in the majors (1956) was also Jackie Robinson's. The two trailblazing second basemen signed by Branch Rickey were also linked in terms of tragedy: Both died young. Robinson succumbed to a heart attack in 1972 at the age of 53. Roberts was killed by a drunk driver in 1969. He was 40.

THE LONGEST NIGHT

After 26 innings, 26 runs and 19 pitchers, the Pirates and Houston managed nothing better than a split of an Aug. 9, 1963, doubleheader. Aug. *9-10* doubleheader, that is.

The nightcap ended in the morning—2:30 a.m., to be exact—making it the latest-finishing game in Bucs history. The original crowd of 9,420 had dwindled to about 300 when Roberto Clemente drilled a bases-loaded single off Dick Drott to give Pittsburgh a 7-6 victory in 11 innings.

"They managed to make a movie out of The Longest Day," noted Les Biederman of the *Pittsburgh Press,* "but it would require a great deal of imagination to make even one good ball game out of the longest night in the history of Forbes Field."

The twinbill began an hour late (7:05 p.m.) because of rain. The first game went 15 innings and lasted three hours, 58 minutes, with Houston winning 7-6 when former Pirate Howie Goss doubled, advanced to third on a sacrifice and scored on Johnny Weekly's grounder.

The second game didn't start until 11:20 p.m. Johnny Logan drew a walk to start the winning rally, Manny Mota and Bob Bailey singled and, after a force at home, Clemente singled to end The Longest Night.

Q Which famous entertainer was part owner of the Pirates from 1946 until his death in 1977?

A Singer-actor Bing Crosby.

Q This player slugged an eighth-inning home run in Game 7 of the 1960 World Series that was arguably as significant as Bill Mazeroski's decisive blast an inning later. Name him.

A Catcher Hal Smith, whose three-run shot off Jim Coates capped a five-run uprising that wiped out a 7-4 deficit and sent the Forbes Field fans into a frenzy.

"It just felt like another home run until I rounded second base and started for third and saw the people," said Smith. "They were on top of the dugout. Then it dawned on me how important it was."

Unfortunately for Smith, the Yankees' game-tying rally in the top of the ninth and Maz's homer in the bottom half of the inning stole his thunder. He went from possible World Series hero to World Series footnote in a matter of minutes. Former teammate Dick Groat once called Smith's blow "the most forgotten home run in baseball history."

Q This pitcher won 124 games in his career, eight with the Bucs in 1976. But he's perhaps best remembered for a save—one that took place *off* the field. Name him.

A George "Doc" Medich, who rode to the rescue as a member of the Texas Rangers on July 17, 1978, when a fan sitting behind the Orioles dugout at Baltimore's Memorial Stadium suffered a heart attack.

"I was running in the outfield before the game when I heard the public address announcement asking for a doctor," said Medich, who was then a medical student. "[Teammate] Dock Ellis told me someone was having a heart attack. When I went into the stands, I could feel the man had no palpable pulse and there was no spontaneous movement."

Using mouth-to-mouth resuscitation and heart massage, Medich revived 61-year-old Germain Languth, a resident of nearby Pasadena, Md.

Q Which Pirate hit the most home runs in a given World Series?

A Willie Stargell, who slugged three in the 1979 Fall Classic against Baltimore—the only long balls hit by Pittsburgh in the Series. That surpassed the team record of two shared by Fred Clarke (1909), Bill Mazeroski (1960), Roberto Clemente (1971) and Bob Robertson (1971). Stargell's three homers also represent the Bucs' career World Series record.

Q Who was Yellowhorse?

A Moses "Chief" Yellowhorse was a Pawnee Indian who served as the Bucs' bullpen ace in 1921 and 1922, compiling an 8-4 record (5-0 in relief). During those seasons—and even years later—cries of "Put in Yellowhorse" would ring out at Forbes Field when the opposition mounted a late-innings threat.

Q True or false: Honus Wagner, the premier shortstop of his time, once committed 60 errors in a season.

A True. Wagner was charged with 60 errors in 1905 and made 40 or more 11 other times in his career.

Of course, players had to contend with uneven surfaces, tiny gloves and less forgiving official scorers back in the early days of baseball. Hence the inflated error totals compiled by even the most accomplished fielders.

Wagner's numbers are especially misleading. He covered a lot of ground, was deceptively quick, gobbled up balls with his huge hands and had a slingshot arm.

"He had the swiftness of a Phil Rizzuto, the agility of a Rabbit Maranville, the anticipatory sense of a Lou Boudreau, the range of a Marty Marion, the shovel hands of an Eddie Miller and the throwing arm of a Travis Jackson," wrote Arthur Daley of *The New York Times*. All but Miller later joined Wagner in Cooperstown.

Said long-time New York Giants manager John McGraw, "The only way to get the ball past Honus Wagner is to hit it eight feet over his head."

And about those errors: Five major league shortstops actually exceeded Wagner's total in 1905. Ed Abbaticchio of the Boston Beaneaters led the big leagues with 75, followed by Freddy Parent of the Boston Pilgrims (66), Washington's Joe Cassidy (66), Brooklyn's Phil Lewis (66) and Bobby Wallace of the Browns (62).

The big league record for single-season miscues by a shortstop was established in 1890 by Bill Shindle of Philadelphia in the Players League—115.

Q Whose wild pitch enabled George Foster to score the winning run in Game 5 of the 1972 National League Championship Series, handing the Reds the pennant?

A Bob Moose. Manager Bill Virdon called on Dave Giusti to protect a 3-2 ninth-inning lead, but Johnny Bench's leadoff home run tied the score. When Tony Perez and Denis Menke followed with singles, Virdon summoned Moose.

Foster, running for Perez, advanced to third on a fly and then scored when Moose's two-out slider bounced in front of the plate and shot over catcher Manny Sanguillen's shoulder.

"It was a study in horror," wrote Bob Smizik of the *Pittsburgh Press*. "The little white ball was out of control. First it hit the dirt, then it bounced high into the air and careened madly to the screen."

Foster gleefully raced down the baseline, dashing the Pirates' dream of a second straight World Series appearance.

Q Until Moose came along, who uncorked the most famous—and most costly—wild pitch in Pirates history?

APittsburgh-born John Miljus, who hurled a delivery over catcher Johnny Gooch's head in Game 4 of the 1927 World Series, enabling Earle Combs to score the run that gave the Yankees the championship.

Combs walked to open the bottom of the ninth, moved to second when Mark Koenig beat out an attempted sacrifice bunt and scampered to third on a wild pitch. Babe Ruth was then passed intentionally, filling the bases.

Miljus regrouped momentarily, striking out Lou Gehrig and Bob Meusel. But his second wild pitch of the inning with Tony Lazzeri at the plate enabled Combs to trot home with the run that gave New York a 4-3 victory and a World Series sweep.

QThis infielder spent 11 years in the major leagues and appeared in 59 games with the Pirates of the 1950s. But his fame grew after he left baseball for Hollywood and became an actor. Name him.

AJohn Berardino, who starred as Chief of Staff Dr. Steve Hardy in the daytime soap *General Hospital* for 33 years—after dropping the second "r" from his name.

Berardino also appeared with Pirates teammate Catfish Metkovich in *The Winning Team,* a 1952 film biography of pitching great Grover Cleveland Alexander that starred Ronald Reagan and Doris Day. Berardino's acting career actually predated his baseball career: He appeared in the silent "Our Gang" comedies as a child.

SWEET RELIEF

Seldom does a pitcher want to come out of a game. But on July 23, 1930, Heinie Meine was gazing into the Pirates dugout with pleading eyes, hoping for relief—both figurative and literal.

He was getting hammered mercilessly by the Brooklyn Dodgers, but manager Jewel Ens made no move to the bullpen. At least not until Meine had allowed 10 consecutive hits to set a National League record and tie the major league mark.

The sixth inning that day began innocently enough. Meine retired Mickey Finn on a fly, yielded a single to Al Lopez and struck out Jumbo Elliott. Then the proverbial roof caved in.

Johnny Frederick singled, Wally Gilbert slugged a three-run homer, Babe Herman followed with a home run, Del Bissonette and Rube Bressler singled and scored on Glenn Wright's triple, Finn delivered an RBI double and Lopez and Elliott singled. The Bucs turned the 10th consecutive hit—

a single to left by Frederick—into the third out when Lopez was cut down at the plate !

Meine allowed 14 runs and 19 hits in his six innings of work. Brooklyn won the game, 19-6.

Q These two infielders were members of the 1952 consensus All-America basketball team, but three years later they were teammates in a real sense, playing with the Pirates. Name them.

A Shortstop Dick Groat and second baseman Johnny O'Brien.

Groat, who was, according to Richard Deitsch of *Sports Illustrated*, blessed with "hands as soft as a lullaby and a jump shot as straight and true as June Cleaver," scored 1,886 points during his career at Duke University, a prolific total for the time. He pumped in 831 points as a junior—still the single-season school standard—and his single-game record of 48 points wasn't eclipsed until Danny Ferry scored 58 against Miami (Fla.) on Dec. 10, 1988.

Groat was selected as the College Player of the Year in 1951 after averaging 26.0 points and 7.6 assists per game. He became the first basketball player in school history to have his uniform number (10) retired.

O'Brien, who starred at Seattle University, repeated as an All-American in 1953. Eddie O'Brien, Johnny's twin brother and Seattle backcourt mate, also played with the Bucs. In fact, all three ex-basketball whizzes were Pirates teammates from 1955 to 1958.

Q This Philadelphia outfielder became only the fourth player in major league history to wallop four home runs in a game when he bludgeoned the Bucs on July 10, 1936—at spacious Forbes Field, no less. Name him.

A Chuck Klein, who played briefly with the Pirates (85 games in 1939) after winning four National League home run crowns with the Phillies.

Klein clubbed "four whining drives into the lower tier of the right field stands," according to Chet Smith of the *Pittsburgh Press*. His fourth homer, a solo shot leading off the 10th inning, broke a 6-6 tie and sparked Philadelphia to a 9-6 victory.

Incredibly, he just missed another home run in the second inning. Paul Waner gloved Klein's towering drive with his back against the right field wall.

Q Which Pirate drilled a two-run double off Washington's Walter Johnson in the eighth inning of Game 7 to give Pittsburgh a 9-7 victory and the 1925 World Series?

A Kiki Cuyler, whose shot down the right field line in the drizzle and late-afternoon gloom at Forbes Field snapped a 7-7 tie. Eddie Moore and Carson Bigbee, who had delivered a game-tying double moments before, scored on Cuyler's two-bagger, sending a crowd of 42,856 into a state of delirium and dethroning the defending world champions.

"Kiki Cuyler's timely smack upon the apple's nose knocked in the runs that made the mighty throng stand up and scream and turned the boast of Washington into an empty dream," wrote Edward F. Balinger in the *Pittsburgh Post*.

The subsequent city-wide celebration was the "wildest since Armistice Day," according to the *Pittsburgh Press*.

Q Who sang the national anthem before the Pirates' first game at Three Rivers Stadium on July 16, 1970?

A Jazz great Billy Eckstine, a Pittsburgh native. The bebop vocalist and trombonist, whose popularity reached its zenith in the late 1940s, earned 11 gold records during his career. His hit songs included *Body and Soul, My Foolish Heart, Blue Moon, Prisoner of Love, I Apologize* and *Fools Rush In*.

Q Pitchers Al Jackson, Bobby Shantz and Jim Umbricht, outfielders Roman Mejias and Joe Christopher and catcher Hal Smith all became ex-Pirates on Oct. 10, 1961. What occurred on that date?

A They were selected by New York and Houston in the National League's first expansion draft. The Mets chose Jackson and Christopher, while the Colt .45s, as the Astros were then known, picked Shantz, Umbricht, Smith and Mejias.

Q This Pirate stole 31 consecutive bases without getting caught during the 1922 season, a major league record that stood for 53 years. Name him.

A Center fielder Max Carey, who swiped a National League-best 51 bases in 53 attempts, a percentage (.962) no league leader has ever matched. Davey Lopes of the Dodgers finally eclipsed Carey's record streak in 1975, when he stole 38 consecutive bases.

Second baseman Tony Womack broke Carey's team mark in 1997, swiping 32 in a row before Mike DiFelice of the Cardinals gunned him down at second base on July 4.

Q How many times did Carey lead the league in steals?

A 10, a National League record. Rickey Henderson holds the major league mark of 12.

Q Name the first Pirate to earn National League Most Valuable Player honors.

A Right fielder Paul Waner, who in 1927 won the League Award, a forerunner to today's Baseball Writers Association of America MVP award. The first Pirate MVP selected under the auspices of the BBWAA was shortstop Dick Groat in 1960.

Q The position player who finished second to Groat in that year's MVP balloting did not bat .300, did not slug 20 home runs, did not drive in 100 runs. But his contributions to the cause could never be measured by statistics. Name him.

A Third baseman Don Hoak, nicknamed "The Tiger" for his fierce temperament.

Hoak's leadership was instrumental in the team's success. Roy Terrell of *Sports Illustrated* called the fiery ex-Marine "the lash that peels the skin off Pirate backs if they dare let down."

For the record, Hoak batted .282 in 1960 with 16 homers, 79 RBIs and a team-high 97 runs.

LITTLE HELP

The interference of a small boy, described by the *Pittsburg Post* as "brave and loyal," helped the Pirates win a game on May 3, 1899. Down 6-1 to Louisville entering the bottom of the ninth, the Bucs scored six times to pull out a stunning 7-6 victory.

According to the *Pittsburg Commercial Gazette*, "The finish was the most remarkable ever seen on the grounds, or any other grounds for that matter, and the best of all was that it was strong enough to enable the locals to win and send the spectators home in a fine humor to supper."

The visiting Colonels were not in such a fine humor. They were one out from victory when the unidentified youngster stepped forward and, without so much as picking up a bat, aided the Pirates' cause.

"Pittsburg needed two runs to tie, and [Jack] McCarthy and a small boy who stood at the right field bleachers fence near the score board supplied the desired number," the *Pittsburg Press* noted. "McCarthy's part of the performance was in driving the ball along the right line [sic]; the boy did the rest."

As the ball skipped toward him, the lad opened the gate through which the Pirates passed en route to their locker room and then closed it, effectively creating a roadblock for right fielder Charlie Dexter.

"The excited Dexter fumbled with the latch for a few seconds, then got into the small garden which surrounds the club house and instituted a search for the boy and the ball, but neither could be found," the *Press* reported. "In the meantime, [Jesse] Tannehill and McCarthy had crossed the plate and the score was tied in a knot."

A swarm of irate Louisville players descended on umpires Oyster Burns and Billy Smith, but their arguments fell on deaf ears. The Colonels' pain intensified moments later when Tom McCreery circled the bases with a game-winning inside-the-park home run.

Unlike McCarthy's, this one required no special assistance.

Q This Pirates catcher—the son of a former big league catcher—made a phenomenal jump from Class AA ball to the major league All-Star game in less than a year. Name him.

A Jason Kendall, who was selected for the 1996 Midsummer Classic at the age of 22, only a year removed from a season with the Carolina Mudcats of the Double-A Southern League. Kendall caught two innings of the National League's 6-0 victory at Philadelphia, but did not bat. He was the first rookie in Pirates history to participate in the All-Star game.

"I was just hoping he'd hold his own," said Fred Kendall of his son's first season in the majors. "If you think about it, how many players come to the big leagues from Double-A and make the All-Star team the first year? That amazes me. It's unbelievable."

Fred Kendall, now a roving minor league catching instructor with the Reds, spent 12 seasons in the big leagues with the Padres, Indians and Red Sox (1969-80) and later coached for the Tigers (1996-98).

Q Name the only player in Pirates history to win the Heisman Trophy, presented annually to the premier college football player in the land.

A Vic Janowicz, who appeared in 83 games as a catcher and third baseman for the 1953 and 1954 Bucs. Janowicz won the Heisman as a triple-threat halfback at Ohio State in 1950.

"He did our field goal kicking, our punting, our quick kicking, was as fine a single-wing halfback as I have seen, did all our passing and was truly a great blocker," recalled Wes Fesler, his coach in 1950. "On defense he played safety. He was absolutely great. He excelled in every phase of the game."

Janowicz, then a junior, led the 6-3 Buckeyes in rushing (314 yards), passing (557 yards and 12 touchdowns), total offense (871 yards), field goals (3), scoring (65 points) and punting.

What's ironic is that a Heisman winner made the big-time as a baseball player before reaching the big-time in football. Janowicz debuted with the Washington Redskins in 1954 and a year later finished second to Detroit's Doak Walker in the NFL scoring race. A promising career came to an abrupt end in 1956 when Janowicz was involved in a near-fatal auto accident during training camp.

The only other Heisman winner to play major league baseball? Bo Jackson, who earned college football's top individual honor in 1985 as an Auburn running back. Jackson debuted in the big leagues less than a year later, with the Royals. He also played with the White Sox and Angels during his eight-year career.

Like Janowicz, Jackson also played in the NFL. He spent four seasons with the Los Angeles Raiders (1987-90) before a hip injury forced him to focus his energies solely on baseball.

Q Who was the first player to clear the 86-foot high right field grandstand at Forbes Field with a batted ball?

Boston Braves outfielder Babe Ruth. Then 40, Ruth slammed the last three home runs of his career on May 25, 1935, with the third—No. 714—clearing the roof and traveling an estimated 550 to 600 feet.

The slugger who revolutionized the game with thunderclap home runs had lamented, "It's hell to get older," but he turned back the clock that day in Pittsburgh and staged an electrifying last hurrah. He would retire a week later.

Noted *The Boston Globe*, "The great man Ruth took Pittsburgh to his massive bosom today and sent 10,000 gabbing fans out of the ballpark convinced that the Bam's legs may be spavined, his body reaching the stage of senility and his glorious major league career in the sunset stage, but his eagle eye, his coordinated swings are just as effective as they were in the days when he was the greatest home run king of them all."

Ruth clubbed his last two home runs off Guy Bush. The second made an indelible impression on the Pirates pitcher.

"I never saw a ball hit so hard," Bush said, recalling Ruth's titanic blow years later. "He was fat and old, but he still had that great swing. Even when he missed, you could hear the bat go swish. I can't remember anything about the first home run he hit off me that day. I guess it was just another homer. But I can't forget that last one. It's probably still going."

Q Who was the second player—and first Pirate—to clear the right field roof at Forbes Field?

A Outfielder Ted Beard, who certainly didn't look the part of a power hitter: He stood 5-8 and weighed 165 pounds. Fact is, Beard *wasn't* a long-ball threat. He hit only six home runs in his seven major league seasons, five of them spent in Pittsburgh.

Beard launched his tape-measure shot on July 16, 1950, against the Braves' Bob Hall.

"I felt strong that day," he recalled 45 years later. "The first time up I hit a line drive to the right fielder. The next time up I got it up in the air and it just kept going."

To the roof and beyond. Ironically, a teammate of Beard's—catcher Ray Mueller—had witnessed Ruth's epic blast as a Boston rookie in 1935.

Q Which Pirate became the first pitcher to lead the league in earned run average while toiling for a last-place team?

A Bob Friend, who compiled a 2.84 ERA (and a 14-9 record) for a woeful 1955 club that finished deep in the National League basement, 38½ games behind the pennant-winning Dodgers.

Q Which Pirates catcher played basketball on Duquesne University's 1955 NIT title team?

A Dave Ricketts, who appeared in 14 games for the 1970 Bucs and served as a Pittsburgh coach the next three seasons. His brother Dick also played on that Duquesne team—he was an All-America selection, in fact—and also reached the major leagues, as a pitcher with the Cardinals. Dick played three seasons of NBA basketball in the 1950s with the Rochester/Cincinnati Royals and the St. Louis Hawks.

Q Which Pirate slugged the most postseason home runs in a given year?

A Bob Robertson, who hit six in 1971—four against San Francisco in the National League Championship Series and two against Baltimore in the World Series—to set a single-season major league standard. Robertson's record was tied by Philadelphia's Lenny Dykstra in 1993 and Ken Griffey Jr. of Seattle in 1995.

Willie Stargell threatened the record in 1979, slamming five postseason homers. Richie Hebner ranks third on the Pirates' list with three in 1971.

Q Which Pirate has hit the most career postseason home runs?

A Stargell, with seven. He clubbed three in the 1979 World Series and two each in the 1974 and 1979 National League Championship Series.

Robertson ranks second with six, followed by Hebner with four and Roberto Clemente, Al Oliver and Jay Bell with three apiece.

Q Which two members of the 1960 Pirates cut a country-western album in the wake of their World Series triumph?

A Catcher Hal Smith and pitcher Elroy Face, who played nightclubs and made an appearance on Perry Como's television show. The album—*Two Bucs at the Holiday House*—was recorded during a show at the popular Monroeville establishment and featured songs such as *Cross Your Heart With Love* and *Bells, Bells*.

"I guess you could say they're collectors' items," Face said. "We sure didn't sell many."

Smith, Face and pitcher Harvey Haddix often performed impromptu concerts in the Pirates clubhouse during the 1960 season.

A Terrific Transformation

J ohn Coleman was one of the more remarkable members of the first Pirates team in 1887, deserving of acclaim simply for keeping his career alive after an abominable big league debut in 1883.

Coleman established major league records by losing 48 games and surrendering 544 runs and 772 hits (in 538⅓ innings) that year for last-place Philadelphia, which won fewer games (17) than 10 National League *pitchers*. The 20-year-old right-hander accounted for 12 of those victories.

Incredibly enough, Coleman's batting average (.234) that year surpassed his winning percentage (.200). Convinced his future was in hitting baseballs, not throwing them, Coleman abandoned the mound for the outfield.

He joined Pittsburgh's American Association team in 1886 and, after the team shifted to the NL in 1887, earned a starting berth in right field. Coleman batted .293 while pacing the club in hits (139) and tying for the team lead in RBIs (54).

Q Only two Pirates pitchers have won Cy Young honors since the award was first presented in 1956. Name them.

A Vernon Law (20-9) in 1960 and Doug Drabek (22-6) in 1990. Steve Blass finished second in the 1972 balloting, though far behind recipient Steve Carlton.

Q Who is the only player in Pirates history to repeat as the National League MVP?

A Left fielder Barry Bonds, who won the award in 1990 and again in 1992. He finished a close second—274 points to 259, one of the smallest margins ever—to Atlanta third baseman Terry Pendleton in 1991.

Bonds became a three-time winner in 1993, his first season as a member of the San Francisco Giants. He thereby joined an elite fraternity: Only seven other players have claimed MVP honors on three occasions since the Baseball Writers Association of America began selecting recipients in 1931.

The other three-time winners are Jimmie Foxx (1932, 1933, 1938), Joe DiMaggio (1939, 1941, 1947), Stan Musial (1943, 1946, 1948), Yogi Berra (1951, 1954, 1955), Roy Campanella (1951, 1953, 1955), Mickey Mantle (1956, 1957, 1962) and Mike Schmidt (1980, 1981, 1986). All seven are in the Hall of Fame.

Q This Pirates pitcher won a franchise-record 36 games in 1893, a total no major league left-hander has matched since. Name him.

A Frank Killen, who posted a 36-14 record that season, his first with the Bucs. Killen had been acquired from the Washington Senators in the offseason.

Q That was not the last time a Pirates pitcher would win at least 30 games. Name the team's most recent 30-game winner.

A Killen. He finished 30-18 in 1896 to lead the National League in victories for a second time. Killen went 27-34 for the duration of his stay in Pittsburgh.

Q Pirates general manager Branch Rickey drafted Roberto Clemente from the Dodgers' Montreal farm club following the 1954 season. How much did Rickey pay for the future Hall of Famer?

A $4,000. Clemente made his major league debut the following April— against the Dodgers.

Q This Pirates hurler hooked up with Rube Marquard of the Giants in a classic pitchers' duel at Forbes Field on July 17, 1914. New York won 3-1 in 21 innings, at that time the longest game in National League history. Who worked 21 innings for naught?

A Babe Adams. Larry Doyle's two-run inside-the-park homer with two outs in the 21st pinned the defeat on Adams, who yielded only 12 hits and did not walk a batter. That marathon contest ranks as the longest home game in Pirates history.

Q The brother of which renowned author played briefly with the Pirates?

A Oufielder Romer "Reddy" Grey, younger brother of Zane Grey, appeared in one game for the pennant-bound 1903 Bucs. He singled and drew a walk in four trips to the plate.
  Reddy hit .320 in a nine-year minor league career and won home run titles in the Inter-State League, with Findlay, Ohio, in 1895 (Zane was a teammate) and the Eastern League, with Buffalo and Rochester, in 1901.
  Zane played two seasons of minor league ball, batting .323 with five home runs, before focusing full-time on writing. He authored 89 books, most of them western adventures, although he did occasionally utilize

baseball themes. In fact, Romer was one of the outfielders upon whom Zane's novel *The Redheaded Outfield* was based.

Q Who threw the first pitch in the first game at Three Rivers Stadium on July 16, 1970?

A Dock Ellis, who tossed a strike to Cincinnati leadoff batter Ty Cline. Cline eventually grounded out to second baseman Bill Mazeroski, who had fielded the last ball hit at Forbes Field.

Q Which player slugged the Pirates' first home run at Three Rivers Stadium?

A Willie Stargell, who launched a solo shot off Cincinnati's Gary Nolan in the sixth inning of the inaugural game.

Stargell earned $1,000 for his feat. Fred Babcock of the Babcock Lumber Company had promised that sum to the first Pirate who homered in the new stadium. The Reds' Tony Perez, the first player to homer at Three Rivers—his two-run blast came an inning earlier—received nothing.

JUST BLOWING SMOKE

P ittsburgh used to be known as the Smoky City, but on the final day of the 1902 season, it was the Cincinnati Reds who polluted the air with smoke—and made a travesty of the game.

The Pirates, who had long since wrapped up the pennant, desperately wanted to play because they needed a victory to eclipse the major league record for wins in a season—102, which they shared with the 1892 and 1898 Boston Beaneaters.

The Reds objected, citing the cold, drizzly conditions. But Pittsburgh owner Barney Dreyfuss insisted the teams go on with the show. And what a show it was: The fourth-place Reds made a mockery of the proceedings.

Player-manager Joe Kelley used three left-handers in the infield, sent three players to the mound who had no previous pitching experience and stuck rookie hurler Harry Vickers behind the plate. Vickers wound up setting a modern major league record for passed balls with six. Not that the Reds cared.

"The whole team staggered around like toughs who had a grievance against good society," noted the *Pittsburg Post*. "They smoked cigarettes with brazen affrontery, Kelley, [Mike] Donlin and [Cy] Seymour blowing the smoke into the air offensively. One of Seymour's stockings hung over his shoe and Donlin wore his cap recklessly on the side of his head.

"Kelley walked into the box with a cigarette in his mouth and puffed away while the ball was being pitched. Vickers, behind the bat, had six passed balls, which seemed to give the Reds great pleasure. He sometimes raised a mirthful howl from his fellows by blowing his nose before going after the ball and using his handkerchief with great care and deliberation."

The Pirates set their record—they won by an 11-2 score—but the Reds had the last laugh.

Q Before coming to the Pirates, Roberto Clemente played left field for the Santurce Cangrejeros (Crabbers), the Puerto Rican Winter League champions of 1954-55. Which future Hall of Famer played alongside Clemente in center?

A Willie Mays, fresh off his MVP season with the world champion New York Giants. Negro Leagues veteran Bob Thurman, who, like Clemente, would make his major league debut that April, started in right field.

Clemente hit .355 as Santurce won not only the league title, but the subsequent Caribbean Series as well. He and Thurman are both members of the Puerto Rico Professional Baseball Hall of Fame.

Q Ground was broken for construction of Three Rivers Stadium on April 25, 1968, and the first game was played on July 16, 1970, a span of nearly 27 months. From the start of construction to the first game, how many months were required to build Forbes Field?

A Four. Construction began on March 1, 1909, and the Pirates and Cubs played the first game there on June 30. The *Pittsburg Press* hailed the new ballpark as "the world's greatest amusement palace."

Q On Sept. 16, 1975, this Pirate became the first National Leaguer in 83 years to bang out seven hits in a game. Name him.

A Second baseman Rennie Stennett, who went 7-for-7 (four singles, two doubles and a triple) in a 22-0 rout of the Cubs at Wrigley Field. "I thought some day I might get five hits in a game," he said. "But I never dreamt I'd get seven."

Stennett went 3-for-5 the next night at Philadelphia to tie the modern National League record for most hits in consecutive nine-inning games.

The only previous seven-hit performance in league history occurred on June 10, 1892, when Baltimore catcher Wilbert Robinson—a future Hall of Famer—went 7-for-7 against St. Louis.

Three American League players have collected at least seven hits in a game, but they each needed extra innings. John Burnett of Cleveland went 9-for-11 in an 18-inning loss to Philadelphia on July 10, 1932, Detroit's Rocky Colavito was 7-for-10 in a 22-inning loss to New York on June 24, 1962, and Detroit's Cesar Gutierrez was 7-for-7 in a 12-inning victory over Cleveland on June 21, 1970.

Q Which would-be base stealer did shortstop Honus Wagner purportedly tag in the mouth in Game 1 of the 1909 World Series?

A Ty Cobb. The tale of how Detroit's brash stolen base champion shouted to Wagner, "Hey, Krauthead, I'm coming down," fits the image we have of Cobb, an intimidating presence on the basepaths who usually came in with spikes high.

The tale has been repeated so often it's been accepted as truth, but the facts simply don't support it. Cobb did try to swipe second base in the fifth inning of the opener—he was safe—but there was no confrontation of any sort.

Cobb later admitted he had too much respect for Wagner to intentionally spike him. And Wagner no doubt realized the folly of inciting Cobb—as fierce a competitor as ever stepped onto a diamond—by planting a tag on his chops.

While Wagner didn't manhandle Cobb, the Pirates' pitchers certainly did. He was held to a .231 average, well below the .377 he hit during the season en route to the third of his record 12 batting crowns. What's more, Cobb was held to two steals after swiping a major league-leading 76 bases that year.

Q Who was the on-deck batter when Bill Mazeroski launched his World Series-winning home run in 1960?

A Dick Stuart, who was sent up to pinch hit for pitcher Harvey Haddix. When Maz connected, teammates rushed to the plate to greet him. Said Stuart, "I almost got trampled to death."

Q Who holds the Pirates record for most home runs hit in a season by a pitcher?

A Emerson "Pink" Hawley, who slugged five home runs and batted .308 in 1895, his first season with the club. Hawley fared well on the mound, too, compiling a 31-22 record. Only Cy Young had more victories (35) in the National League that year.

Q Who holds the single-season team record for home runs by a catcher?

A Jim Pagliaroni, who hit 17 in 1965.

Q Who holds the franchise record for most home runs in a season by a shortstop?

A Arky Vaughan, with 19 in 1935. Vaughan not only established a team record for a player at that position; he established a team record for a player at *any* position. Vaughan eclipsed by one the modest franchise standard of 18 set by Kiki Cuyler and Glenn Wright in 1925.

His power surge was certainly uncharacteristic: Discounting 1935, Vaughan averaged only six home runs a season during his 14-year Hall of Fame career.

Generally, Pirates shortstops have upheld the image of players at their position as lightweight power hitters who pack all the punch of Popeye before his spinach (think Rafael Belliard). In fact, in a 10-year span starting in 1972, the team's No. 1 shortstops clubbed eight home runs—total.

Belliard, by the way, cracked one homer in 1,051 career at bats with the Pirates (1982-90). But even that anemic effort enabled the diminutive Dominican to outstrip countryman Frank Taveras. A starter for five seasons (1974-78), Taveras never did blast a ball over the fence in a Pittsburgh uniform. He managed one home run in 2,476 career at bats as a Pirate.

His lone homer was an inside-the-park blow—on a line drive inside first base—against Cincinnati's Doug Capella on Aug. 5, 1977. The ball caromed away from Reds right fielder Ken Griffey as Taveras circled the bases with a grand slam, highlighting a 10-6 Pittsburgh victory.

Q Name the only player to hold single-season team home run records at two positions.

A Frank Thomas, who slugged 30 as a center fielder in 1953 and 35 in 1958 after moving to third base.

THE UNEXPECTED MASTERPIECE

B ruce Kison came within one pitch of a no-hitter the afternoon of June 3, 1979, an incredible feat given that he'd pitched in relief the night before.

Kison stepped in as an emergency starter and responded with a one-hit performance in a 7-0 victory over San Diego.

"He was just unbelievable," said Padres manager Roger Craig. "He didn't even know he was going to start, and he pitches like that. I think that would've been a first—a guy pitching in relief one night and then pitching a no-hitter the next day."

Manager Chuck Tanner found himself in a real bind when Don Robinson's shoulder stiffened during pre-game warm-ups. He tabbed Kison, who hurled a scoreless inning in a 3-1 loss 16 hours before. Kison was so sure he wouldn't be pitching that he ate a sandwich 30 minutes before gametime.

"He was rested the most," Tanner explained. "I hoped he could give us a few innings. Bert Blyleven volunteered to pitch two or three innings in the middle, then I could use Kent Tekulve as long as I could and finish up the game with Grant Jackson or Enrique Romo."

But Blyleven, Tekulve, Jackson and Romo never budged from the bench. Armed with a paralyzing slider, Kison was magnificent. He carried a no-hitter into the eighth inning before Barry Evans, a .197 hitter, ripped a two-out grounder past lunging third baseman Phil Garner for a double. The ball tipped Garner's glove as it bounced past.

"I almost had it," he said. "The problem was, when it hit the dirt it took off toward the line. If it had been a one-run game [Pittsburgh led by seven at the time], I would have been playing the line and I would have fielded it easily."

As Evans pulled into second, official scorer Dan Donovan flashed "hit" on the scoreboard. The fans at Three Rivers Stadium did not boo the ruling; they stood and applauded Kison for coming within four outs of a no-hitter. But the pitcher took umbrage at the decision, shaking his fist and glowering at the press box after retiring Dave Winfield to end the game.

Reporters encountered an agitated Kison in the locker room afterwards. Instead of euphoria over winning a one-hitter, he was angered over "losing" a no-hitter.

"I'm unhappy for a very personal reason," Kison said. "It's a once-in-a-lifetime situation. I just wanted it so bad. I may never get the chance again. I came close. Close, but no cigar."

Kison later discussed the decision at length with Donovan and ultimately accepted his ruling. It might not have been a no-hitter he threw against San Diego, but it was still one of the more masterful exhibitions of pitching in Pittsburgh history, given the circumstances.

Said teammate Bill Robinson, "It was the guttiest performance I've ever seen."

Q No one has slugged fewer home runs and yet led the Pirates in that category than rookie first baseman Jim Nealon in 1906 and catcher Bill Fischer in 1917. How many homers did they hit?

A Three. Incredibly, Fischer accounted for one-third of his team's home run total in 1917. The Bucs slugged a franchise-low nine in 157 games.

Q Ed Doheny compiled a 16-8 record for the Pirates during the 1903 season, but he did not appear in the World Series. Why?

A He was committed to an insane asylum not long before the Fall Classic began.

Doheny was institutionalized in Danvers, Mass.—located less than 15 miles from Boston, where his teammates opened the Series—after assaulting a man with a castiron stove footrest, knocking him unconscious. He never pitched in the majors again. Doheny was 38-14 in parts of three seasons with Pittsburgh.

Q The Pirates helped bid adieu to which storied baseball landmark in 1957?

A Ebbets Field in Brooklyn. The Bucs lost to the Los Angeles-bound Dodgers 2-0 on Sept. 24 in the last game played on the hallowed grounds at Bedford Avenue and Sullivan Place.

Five days later the Pirates appeared in the final home game in New York Giants history, whipping the San Francisco-bound Giants 9-1 at the Polo Grounds. Unlike Ebbets Field, the Polo Grounds was spared the wrecking ball—at least until after the expansion Mets took up residency in 1962.

Q Which one-time Pittsburgh slugger played in the New York Giants' last game at the Polo Grounds and the New York Mets' first game at the ballpark five years later?

A Frank Thomas, a Pirates first baseman in the Giants' finale and a Mets left fielder when the new New York franchise made its home debut on April 13, 1962—against the Bucs. No other player participated in both milestone games.

Q Roberto Clemente started in more All-Star games—seven—than any other Pirate. Who ranks second on the list?

A Second baseman Bill Mazeroski, who started six. Of course, both had the advantage of playing during a period (1959-62) when two All-Star games were staged each summer.

Incidentally, Clemente appeared in the Midsummer Classic a team-record 14 times.

Q Which Pirates pitcher made the most All-Star appearances?

A Elroy Face, who worked five and two-thirds innings in four Midsummer Classics: 1959 (both games), 1960 and 1961. Face didn't fare particularly well against American League batters, judging by his 9.53 ERA.

Rip Sewell (1943, 1944, 1946) and Bob Friend (1956, 1958, 1960) appeared in three games apiece. Friend owns franchise records for All-Star starts (2), wins (2) and innings pitched (8⅓). In addition, his ERA (1.08) is the best by any Pirates hurler who has worked more than three innings.

Q This Pirate hit nine inside-the-park home runs in 1925, the majors' best single-season total in the post-World War I era. Name him.

A Right fielder Kiki Cuyler, who utilized his speed and Forbes Field's vast expanses to surpass the team record of eight set by Owen "Chief" Wilson in 1911. Only Sam Crawford of the Reds (12 in 1901) ever hit more in a season.

Cuyler finished his career with 18 inside-the-park home runs. Crawford holds the all-time record with 50. Four Pirates rank in the top 10: Tommy Leach, second with 48; Honus Wagner, fourth with 45; Wilson, seventh with 31; and Max Carey, 10th with 28.

Q Who was Dr. Strangeglove?

A Pirates first baseman Dick Stuart. His notorious defensive deficiencies earned him that evocative nickname, a take-off on *Dr. Strangelove*, a popular Peter Sellers movie of the time.

How atrocious was Stuart in the field? Pittsburgh fans once gave him a standing ovation for successfully scooping up a windblown hot dog wrapper at Forbes Field.

Stuart led the National League in errors in all five of his seasons with the Bucs and then, against all odds, actually deteriorated defensively after joining the Red Sox in 1963. He committed a career-high 29 errors that year and followed with 24 in 1964, far and away the worst totals in the American League. Stuart's seven-year "reign of errors" (1958-64) represents a major league record for players at any position.

Small wonder former Pirates manager Bobby Bragan called him "the worst fielder I have ever seen."

BASEBALL'S FIRST MICHAEL JORDAN

C hicago Bulls guard Michael Jordan stunned the sports world in 1993 when he announced his retirement from professional basketball to try his hand at another sport—baseball.

Jordan didn't find much success during his 17-month "sabbatical" from the NBA—he advanced to the Double-A level before deciding to return to the Bulls—but it's unlikely he was much worse than Michael Jordan.

The *other* Michael Jordan, that is. The one who also played baseball in the '90s—the *1890s*.

Michael Henry Jordan, born in 1863—exactly 100 years before Michael Jeffrey Jordan—was arguably the worst hitter among position players in major league history. He was awful even by the pitiful standards of the 1890 Pirates, who finished last in the league in scoring, batting, home runs and slugging percentage. The rookie outfielder fit right in with that motley crew, batting a microscopic .096 (12-for-125).

No wonder he never played again in the majors. To this day, Jordan is saddled with a dubious distinction: Discounting pitchers and catchers, he is the only big leaguer in history with at least 100 career at bats to hit below .100.

Q The Pirates have participated in seven World Series and won five of them, a percentage of .714. How many franchises have a better percentage (minimum of three appearances)?

A None. The Yankees rank second with a .686 figure (24 championships in 35 appearances, both records), followed by the Mets (.667, two titles in three appearances) and the Athletics (.643, nine championships in 14 appearances).

Q Four pitchers have won 20 games four times for the Pirates, but only one did it in consecutive seasons. Name him.

A Hall of Famer Vic Willis, who was acquired from the Boston Pilgrims in December of 1905 after leading the American League in losses (29) for the second year in a row. Willis topped 20 victories in each of his four seasons with the Bucs, winning highs of 23 games in 1906 and 1908.

The Pirates' other four-time 20-game winners are Deacon Phillippe, Jesse Tannehill and Wilbur Cooper.

Q Who hit the ground ball that took a wicked hop and struck Yankees shortstop Tony Kubek in the throat, prolonging a Pirates rally in Game 7 of the 1960 World Series?

A Bill Virdon. A potential double play ball turned into an infield single as a result, opening the doors for a five-run uprising in Pittsburgh's eighth inning that erased a 7-4 deficit.

"There were so many clods of dirt in the infield," said Kubek years later. "Every ball in front of you took a bad hop. It was as fast as an artificial surface, only you got so many bad hops."

The worst coming on the ball hit by Virdon. Wrote Arthur Daley in *The New York Times*, "The grounder, spitefully steered by Dame Fortune, struck a pebble and leaped at Kubek's throat, felling him for a freakish hit."

Myron Cope provided a vivid description of the moment in the *Pittsburgh Post-Gazette:* "The ball hopped higher than Kubek had gauged it and struck him full in the Adam's apple. His mouth flew open, as if he were trying to scream, he clutched his throat with his hands and sagged backwards, like a fighter smashed onto queer street."

Q The highest-scoring game in Pirates history occurred on June 6, 1894, when Pittsburgh bombed Boston. How many runs did the visiting Bucs score that afternoon?

A 27. The Pirates eased to a 27-11 victory, pounding a club-record seven home runs in the process (a mark equaled in 1947). Jacob Stenzel and Lou Bierbauer slugged two homers apiece and Connie Mack, Dennis Lyons and Frank Scheibeck also connected. Bierbauer contributed four of the Bucs' 20 hits and scored five times.

Noted the *Pittsburg Post,* "It was fun for the Pittsburgs, but torture to the spectators, many of whom left, being unable to stand the pain."

The Pirates set their modern scoring record of 24 runs in 1925 at the Cardinals' expense.

Q Although Pirates have won a total of 24 National League batting titles—more than any other franchise—the club once endured a 20-year stretch without one. Which player ended that drought?

A Shortstop Dick Groat, who hit .325 in 1960 to become the Bucs' first batting champion since third baseman Debs Garms won top honors in 1940 with a .355 average.

Although Groat brought a .286 career average into the 1960 season, he didn't consider himself a threat to claim a batting crown. "This is one title," he said, "I never thought I would win."

Q Who was the first pitcher in Pirates history to record more than 200 strikeouts in a season?

A Bob Veale. Not until 1964, when Veale led the National League with 250 strikeouts, did a Pittsburgh hurler top the 200 mark. He fanned 276 batters a year later, establishing a team record that stands to this day.

Veale struck out 200 or more in a season four times, a feat no one else in the team's history has accomplished even once.

Q Match the following Pirates with their given names:

1. Pie Traynor (1920-37)	A. Truett
2. Goose Gossage (1977)	B. Fred
3. Rip Sewell (1938-49)	C. Harold
4. Rocky Nelson (1951, 1959-61)	D. Glenn
5. Dixie Walker (1948-49)	E. Richard

A 1. C   2. E   3. A   4. D   5. B

Q More matches—determine each Pirate's given name:

1. Preacher Roe (1944-47)	A. George
2. Kiki Cuyler (1921-27)	B. Charles
3. Deacon Phillippe (1900-11)	C. Hazen

4. Catfish Metkovich (1951-53)   D. Clarence
5. Ginger Beaumont (1899-1906)   E. Elwin

A 1. E   2. C   3. B   4. A   5. D

Q A final installment of match the names:

1. Vinegar Bend Mizell (1960-62)   A. Forrest
2. Rabbit Maranville (1921-24)   B. Wilmer
3. Arky Vaughan (1932-41)   C. Walter
4. Smoky Burgess (1959-64)   D. George
5. Rube Waddell (1900-01)   E. Floyd

A 1. B   2. C   3. E   4. A   5. D

OUT OF CONTROL

P itcher Steve Blass enjoyed his winningest season in 1972, posting a 19-8 record and leading the division-champion Pirates in victories. Then his career unraveled, for reasons not even Blass can fathom.

This much is known: He managed only three more major league victories. One year Blass was at the top of his game, threatening to become the club's first 20-game winner since Vernon Law in 1960. The next he couldn't even find the plate.

Blass foundered when his control mysteriously vanished: He issued as many walks (84) in 88²/₃ innings during the 1973 season as he had in 249²/₃ innings the year before. Blass finished with a 3-9 record, a 9.85 ERA and precious little confidence.

"It's a very lonely feeling because after a while, none of your teammates knows what to say to you anymore," said Blass, now a Pirates broadcaster. "But mostly it's horribly embarrassing because you're always afraid your next pitch might end up in the hot dog stand. It can be hell just standing on the mound."

Blass tried everything to regain his form: He consulted oculists, threw between starts—sometimes from in front of the mound—underwent hypnosis, did eye-control exercises . . . but nothing worked. Blass made his final major league appearance on April 17, 1974, giving up five hits, seven walks and five earned runs in five innings against Chicago. He was dispatched to the minors, where he spent the remainder of the season.

Manager Danny Murtaugh gave Blass one final opportunity to exorcise his demons in a spring training start against the White Sox on March 24, 1975. He walked eight batters in an agonizing fourth inning and shuffled off the mound for the last time, his career history at the age of 32. He never did figure out what went wrong.

"If I could explain it, I could correct it," Blass said in the midst of his miseries. "I'm almost to the point where I think I was allotted nine years in the big leagues and that was it. It's like somebody decided, you'll fulfill all your dreams, you'll be here nine years and then you're out of here."

Q Who was the Pirates' first Gold Glove winner?

A Second baseman Bill Mazeroski in 1958. The awards for defensive excellence debuted in 1957. Before he was finished, Maz would win eight Gold Gloves, the second-highest total in team history. Right fielder Roberto Clemente was awarded 12, consecutively (1961-72).

Q Three players who never won a single Gold Glove between them share the Pirates record for most league fielding championships won. Name this shortstop, second baseman and catcher.

A Honus Wagner, Claude Ritchey and Al Lopez, who all retired before the Gold Glove awards were inaugurated.

Wagner won four fielding crowns at shortstop toward the end of his career (1912-15), matching the record set by Ritchey, his former double play partner. Ritchey led National League second basemen in 1902, 1903, 1905 and 1906 and added a fifth NL title in 1907 following his trade to Boston. Lopez led the league's catchers in fielding percentage in 1940 and repeated in 1942, 1943 and 1944.

The major league standard for fielding crowns is held by long-time Baltimore Orioles third baseman Brooks Robinson, who claimed 11 in a 16-year span beginning in 1960.

For the record, Pittsburgh's two top Gold Glove recipients won three fielding crowns. Mazeroski reigned as the NL leader at second base in 1960, 1965 and 1966; Clemente never did lead the league.

Q Who was Aunt Minnie?

A The creation of Albert "Rosey" Rowswell, voice of the Pirates from 1936 to 1954.

The fictional Aunt Minnie was "born" in 1938 and lived in an apartment just beyond the outfield wall at Forbes Field. When a Pirate would send a pitch toward the fences, Rowswell would shout, "Get upstairs, Aunt Minnie, and raise the window. Here she [the baseball] comes."

But Aunt Minnie never made it. As the home run cleared the wall, an assistant would drop a tray of bells, nuts and bolts onto the floor, creating a tremendous crash to simulate a window shattering. That was Bob Prince's job when he signed on as Rowswell's sidekick in 1948.

Q On Aug. 31, 1968, Elroy Face tied Walter Johnson's major league record for most pitching appearances with one club (802). How did the Pirates honor Face for this notable achievement?

A They sold him to Detroit, bringing to an abrupt end his 15-year association with the team.

Steve Blass, the starter against Atlanta that afternoon at Forbes Field, retired leadoff batter Felipe Alou and then moved to left field as Face was summoned from the bullpen with great fanfare. He retired Felix Millan on a grounder and then left the game to thunderous applause as Blass returned to the mound to complete an 8-0 victory. Face was sold that day.

Said general manager Joe Brown after reluctantly parting with his ace reliever, "He not only is one of the great pitchers in Pirate history, but one of the great pitchers in the history of baseball. He's given us so many thrills."

Q Who was Nat Moll?

A In the 1920s, before the advent of public address systems, Moll stood behind home plate and "funneled his stentorian voice through a small megaphone to announce batteries and sundry info" at Forbes Field, as *Pittsburgh Post-Gazette* writer Andy Dugo phrased it. Ironically, Moll returned to Forbes Field in the 1970s, overseeing its demolition in his role as a state building inspector.

Q Which pitcher did Paul Waner victimize when he drilled his 3,000th career hit in 1942?

A Rip Sewell of the Pirates. Waner, then with the Braves, had been a teammate of Sewell's with the Bucs from 1938 to 1940.

Q These three brothers—one a future Pirate—made baseball history on Sept. 15, 1963, at Forbes Field when they comprised the entire San Francisco outfield for one inning in a 13-5 Giants win. Name them.

A Felipe (center field), Matty (left) and Jesus (right) Alou. Felipe and Matty had been Giants teammates since 1960. Jesus joined the club in 1963 when he was recalled from Tacoma at the close of the Pacific Coast League season. Matty later spent five years with the Pirates.

Q Which former Pirates pitcher was the last major leaguer to legally throw a spitball?

A Hall of Famer Burleigh Grimes, who won 48 of his 270 games with the Bucs. The spitball was outlawed on Feb. 10, 1920, but the 17 active hurlers who relied heavily on the pitch were allowed to continue. Grimes outlasted the others, finishing his career in 1934.

Q Which Pirate was the first big leaguer paid to endorse baseball equipment?

A Honus Wagner, who supplemented his income in 1904 by endorsing a bat.

STEALTHY STEALER

F red Clarke of the Pirates stole home—and didn't even realize it— during a 1906 game against the Cubs.

Jim Nealon, batting with the bases loaded, took a 3-1 pitch from Mordecai "Three-Finger" Brown to commence an unusual sequence of events. When not a peep was heard from plate umpire Hank O'Day, Clarke trotted home from third and Nealon headed for first, both having assumed the delivery was a ball. But just as Clarke touched home, O'Day blurted out, "Strike two."

Explained the umpire later, "There was a frog in my throat. I couldn't say a word."

Clarke was consequently credited with a leisurely steal of home.

Q Who was the last Pirates pitcher to start an All-Star game?

A Jerry Reuss, who hurled three scoreless innings in the 1975 Midsummer Classic at Milwaukee's County Stadium. He was not involved in the decision.

Q Who was the first Pirates pitcher to win an All-Star game?

A Bob Friend, who hurled three scoreless innings in 1956 at Washington. Friend was also the first Pirates pitcher to start in the Midsummer Classic. He added a second All-Star victory in 1960.

Q Who was the last Pirates pitcher to win an All-Star game?

A Ken Brett. He hurled two scoreless innings of relief in 1974 as the National League prevailed 7-2 at Three Rivers Stadium.

Q What do catchers Joe Garagiola and Toby Atwell, pitchers Howie Pollet and Bob Schultz, outfielders Catfish Metkovich, Bob Addis and Gene Hermanski, first baseman Preston Ward and third baseman George Freese have in common?

A They were the players involved with Ralph Kiner in the blockbuster 10-man deal between the Pirates and Cubs on June 4, 1953. Because the teams were playing that afternoon at Forbes Field, Garagiola, Pollet, Metkovich and Kiner simply walked over to the Chicago clubhouse.

Kiner, recalling the trade years later, called it "the worst moment of my life." He retired two years later at the age of 32 because of back problems.

Q The winningest pitcher in Pirates history managed only a 41-45 record in his first five seasons in Pittsburgh, but he ultimately blossomed into a consistent winner and finished his career with 216 victories, 202 of them with the Bucs. Name him.

A Wilbur Cooper, who pitched for the Pirates from 1912 to 1924. Cooper's breakthrough season was 1917, when he finished 17-11 for a team that thudded into the National League basement with a 51-103 record.

Sam Leever and Babe Adams rank second with 194 wins apiece, followed by Bob Friend (191) and Deacon Phillippe (168).

Q Long before joining the Pirates, this slugger went 5-for-5 with a record-setting five home runs for his Gary, Ind., team in the 1971 Little League World Series. Name him.

A Lloyd McClendon, who took only five swings in that memorable World Series, depositing all five pitches beyond the fence at Lamade Stadium in Williamsport, Pa. McClendon drew intentional walks in his other five plate appearances.

"Lloyd the Legend," as he came to be known, also hurled a three-hitter to pick up the victory in his team's quarterfinal showdown with Lexington, Ky. McClendon slammed two homers in that game, two more in a semifinal win over Madrid, Spain, and another in the title contest against Tainan, Taiwan. Unfortunately, his heroics weren't sufficient to lift Gary to the championship.

McClendon's long-standing record fell in 1995 when Taiwan's Lin Chih-Hsiang slugged six home runs. Lin's record survived for only one year, as countryman Hsieh Chin-Hsiung smashed seven to lead Taiwan to yet another Little League title in 1996. It should be noted that Lin and Hsieh played in five games at Williamsport; McClendon played in three.

McClendon, an outfielder with the Bucs from 1990 to 1994, currently serves the club as its batting coach.

Q Who were Destiny's Darlings?

A The world champion 1960 Pirates, who earned that moniker in honor of their penchant for repeatedly battling back to win games that seemed hopelessly lost. They recorded 23 of their 95 victories that year in the final at bat, 12 with two outs. Surrender was a concept alien to the Bucs of 1960.

"That's the fightingest ball club I've ever seen," said shortstop Dick Groat. "All year we came from behind to win after everybody counted us out. We never knew enough to quit."

An Easter Sunday game against Cincinnati served as a microcosm for the season as a whole. Down 5-0 entering the ninth, the Pirates roared back for a 6-5 victory that sent Reds manager Fred Hutchinson into a clubhouse rage.

"We won ballgames we had no business winning," said pitcher Vernon Law. "It was kind of magical."

For opponents, it was kind of unbelievable.

"That season a lot of teams left Forbes Field shaking their heads," said outfielder Bob Skinner. "They thought they had a win in their pockets."

Until Destiny's Darlings picked them.

Q This Pirates pitcher was such an offensive threat that manager Chuck Tanner once started him in left field. Name him.

A Don Robinson, who batted in the No. 3 slot during the final game of the 1984 season. He went 1-for-3 with an RBI to finish with a .290 average.

The year before, after his season was curtailed by shoulder problems, Robinson reported to the Pirates' Florida Instructional League team, where he played right field on days he didn't pitch. Robinson led the league in home runs (9) and RBIs (35) and hit .313.

He finished his major league career with a .231 average and 13 home runs.

MR. CLEAN

P irates pitcher Larry French reversed the normal sequence during a July 12, 1933, game against Boston. While hurlers are usually sent from the mound to the showers, he was sent from the showers to the mound.

French didn't figure to pitch that day, what with the Bucs leading 8-0 and Heinie Meine working on a two-hitter through eight innings. So he decided to sneak off to the locker room and get an early start on his shower. Bad move.

When the Braves mounted a furious rally, manager George Gibson ordered French to warm up. A clubhouse boy finally located him in the shower, soaked and soaped. By the time French toweled off, redressed and entered the game, Boston had sliced the lead to 8-7.

French yielded a game-tying sacrifice fly to the first batter he faced, but he wound up winning the game when Pittsburgh scored in the 10th. Only then was French able to return to the locker room—and finish his shower in peace.

Q What was unusual about Angelo Encarnacion's balk during the 1995 season?

A Encarnacion wasn't pitching—he was catching. The Pirates rookie was cited under rule Rule 7.05D, which prohibits catchers from touching a ball that's in play with their masks.

Pittsburgh and Los Angeles were locked in a 10-10 tie in the 11th inning of an Aug. 20 game at Dodger Stadium when Encarnacion, after blocking a pitch in the dirt, absent-mindedly scooped it up with his mask and handed it to umpire Brian Gorman. The runner on third, Roberto Kelly, was waved home with the winning run.

Said Pittsburgh coach Rich Donnelly, "I told Angelo he has to be like the Lone Ranger from now on: Never take that mask off. Never. We're gonna glue it to his face."

Q This flame-throwing right-hander led the Pirates in strikeouts in 1977, a remarkable feat given that he was a relief pitcher. Name him.

A Goose Gossage, who fanned 151 batters in 133 innings of work, two short of the National League record for relievers set seven years before by Dick Selma of the Phillies. John Candelaria led the club's starters that season with 133 strikeouts.

Q The most dominating Pittsburgh team of them all won the National League championship by 27 1/2 games over second-place Brooklyn. In what year did the Pirates positively humble the rest of the league?

A 1902. Manager Fred Clarke's club finished 103-36, a franchise-record .741 percentage. Only one team in modern major league history—the 1906 Cubs (.763)—has topped that figure.

The Pirates' 27 1/2-game margin represents a record for the pre-divisional era. Only Cleveland, which won the 1995 American League Central Division crown with a 30-game cushion over second-place Kansas City, has surpassed the Bucs' 1902 achievement.

Q Which former University of Pittsburgh quarterback did the Pirates draft in 1966?

A Fred Mazurek, who led the Panthers to a 9-1 record and a No. 4 ranking nationally as a junior in 1963.

Mazurek was also a standout outfielder at Pitt. In fact, he finished second in the nation with a .484 batting average in 1965. The Twins selected Mazurek in the June amateur draft, but he rejected their contract offer.

Mazurek also turned down the Pirates after they selected him in the secondary phase of the January 1966 draft. By then, he had already put in the first of his two seasons as a flanker-kick returner with the Washington Redskins.

Q This Pirate is the only player in big league history to capture MVP honors during the regular season, the League Championship Series and the World Series. Name him.

A First baseman Willie Stargell, who pulled off an unprecedented trifecta in 1979. No other major leaguer has claimed all three awards in a *career*, much less in a single season.

While Stargell's regular-season numbers were modest compared to those posted by most MVP recipients—32 home runs, 82 RBIs and a .281 average—the voters recognized his role as the Bucs' spiritual leader and a guiding force in the team's charge toward a fifth world championship.

In another unprecedented turn of events, Stargell tied St. Louis first baseman Keith Hernandez for top honors in the regular-season MVP balloting. Hernandez led the National League in batting (.344), runs (116) and doubles (48) and finished second in hits (210).

Q Who made the 27th out in Harvey Haddix's perfect game and later wound up as the winning pitcher—despite allowing 12 hits?

A Lew Burdette, who hurled 13 shutout innings and helped make an undeserving loser of Haddix.

"I told Harvey that I scattered my 12 hits and he bunched his one," said Burdette. "But I was sorry as hell he didn't win it. It was a damn shame Harvey didn't win that game."

After Burdette struck out to end the ninth inning, the 19,194 fans at County Stadium gave Haddix a rousing standing ovation. They could not have imagined that he would toss three more perfect innings—and still end up a loser.

Q Which Pirates Hall of Famer made his All-Star game debut in 1944, at the age of 70?

A Honus Wagner. Then a coach with the Bucs, he was named to the National League coaching staff for the game at Forbes Field. Wagner wrapped up his playing career in 1917, long before *Chicago Tribune* sports editor Arch Ward even conceived the notion of baseball dream teams dueling on the diamond.

Q Which Pirates pitcher died in a car crash on his 29th birthday?

A Bob Moose, who was killed in Martin's Ferry, Ohio, on Oct. 9, 1976, less than a week after completing his 10th season with the club. Moose's car went out of control on a rain-slicked road and collided with another.

The Pirates placed a plaque in the clubhouse honoring Moose, who finished with a 76-71 career record. It reads: "In memory of Bob Moose, a great competitor who had desire, confidence, class and style, but above all, the ability to be color-blind when it came to people from origins different than his own. He never made a show of it, but he had a feeling for people—a feeling that was there no matter what happened on the ball field. He was a pro with a special kind of class."

THE SPYING GAME

B aseball owners often come under fire from fans—for lavishing seven-figure salaries on mediocre players, for raising ticket prices to exorbitant levels, for threatening to relocate franchises.

William Nimick was reviled because he hired detectives. Players and fans alike vilified Nimick in 1887 when he employed operatives to shadow several players suspected of drinking.

During a pregame meeting on June 21, manager Horace Phillips warned players "who have been indulging in lager and whisky a little too freely lately," according to the *Pittsburgh Post*. When Phillips' admonition went unheeded, Nimick took the extraordinary step of hiring detectives to trail his own employees.

In media reports, Nimick painted a picture of players who "led a reckless life" and were guilty of "midnight carousing." The issue came to a head July 5 when outfielders Fred Carroll and Tom Brown and pitcher Ed Morris were caught drinking in Philadelphia and fined $50 apiece.

The *Post* called for the immediate release of the trio. An account of the incident concluded with the following pronouncement: "It will certainly be more credible [sic] to lose with a team of gentlemen than with a number of debauchees."

Brown, who resigned his captaincy over the flap, viewed management's actions as "unjust and tyrannical." The public sided with the players. Fans sympathized with the "boozers," as the *Post* referred to them, and blasted the club's covert activities as reprehensible.

Before long, Nimick removed his spies from the payroll.

Q Who delivered the Pirates' first hit at Forbes Field?

A George Gibson. The Pittsburgh catcher drilled a second-inning single off Ed Ruelbach of the Cubs.

Chicago's Frank Chance was the first player to hit safely at Forbes Field, his first-inning single to center off Vic Willis scoring Johnny Evers with the game's—and the ballpark's—first run. Willis had hit Evers with a pitch to open the inning.

The Cubs won that inaugural game, 3-2.

Q Which current Pirate celebrated a world championship in baseball the same year his wife celebrated an Olympic victory?

A Ed Sprague, who came to the Bucs after signing a free-agent contract on Dec. 15, 1998.

Sprague was a reserve catcher-infielder for the 1992 Toronto Blue Jays, who defeated Atlanta in six games to win their first World Series. His ninth-inning pinch-hit homer off Jeff Reardon decided Game 2.

Two months before, Kristen Babb-Sprague won a gold medal for the United States in synchronized swimming at the Barcelona Games. Sprague had earned an Olympic gold medal of his own as a member of the U.S. team in 1988, when baseball was still a demonstration sport.

Q In 1890 the Pirates played a regular-season home game beyond the borders of Pennsylvania. Where?

A Wheeling, W.Va. On Sept. 22, Pittsburgh dropped an 8-3 decision to the New York Giants at Island Grounds, situated on Wheeling Island in the Ohio River.

The Pirates were such a dismal draw—their total home attendance in 1890 was a paltry 16,064—that team officials regularly took them on the road for home contests. Site shifts were especially common late in the season, when the Bucs were stumbling toward the finish line (and a 23-113 record), unable to attract even triple-figure crowds to Recreation Park.

J. Palmer O'Neil, team president William Nimick's right-hand man, characterized the Pirates' impromptu road show as a noble undertaking designed to bring major league baseball to outlying communities. In reality, it was a desperate attempt to stanch the flow of red ink. The team was willing to play in just about any town where receipts were likely to exceed those at nearly deserted Recreation Park.

The club's decision to shift the Sept. 22 game to Wheeling—located about 45 miles southwest of Pittsburgh—made sense, given that two members of the Giants, shortstop Jack Glasscock and right fielder Jesse Burkett, were natives of the city and were likely to attract fans. Burkett singled, doubled and homered against Pirates' pitcher Bill Day. Glasscock added two hits.

"The sympathy of the spectators was largely with the New Yorkers, for the reason that two of their best players, Jack Glasscock and Jesse Burkett, are Wheeling boys," noted the *Wheeling Intelligencer*. "Nearly one thousand people were present, of whom about one hundred were ladies."

A highlight of the game was Mike Tiernan's unusual home run, which disappeared into "the profuse vegetation" that passed for an outfield. According to an account in the *Wheeling Daily Register*, "The game was played under some slight disadvantages, as the outfield was unkempt and unshaven, the grass being so tall that the ball, and almost the players, frequently got lost. Tiernan knocked one into the tall grass, and while some seven or eight players were on the hunt, he modestly crossed the home plate."

Q Which Pirate inadvertently cost his team an Opening Day victory— because of an untied shoelace?

A Shortstop Frankie Zak, who earned a place in infamy on April 17, 1945. Zak was standing on first base and teammate Al Lopez was perched on second when Cincinnati's Bucky Walters prepared to pitch to Jim Russell.

Zak asked for time when he noticed his lace undone. Umpire John "Ziggy" Sears began shouting and waving his arms frantically, but Walters, Russell and plate ump George Barr didn't notice.

Walters delivered the pitch and Russell blasted it over the center field wall at Crosley Field for an apparent three-run homer. Unfortunately, it didn't count because Zak had called for time. The Pirates scored only one run that inning instead of three, a factor in their 7-6 defeat.

The next day, Zak quipped that he was going to purchase new shoes "with buckles instead of laces."

Q What was significant about Cy Young's 1-0 victory over the Pirates on Sept. 22, 1911?

A It was the last of his major league-record 511 career wins. Young, then pitching for Boston, was 44 at the time.

Q This Hall of Fame first baseman joined the Pirates as a 20-year-old rookie in 1888. In seven and a half seasons with Pittsburgh, he topped 100 RBIs three times, 100 runs four times and batted over .300 five times. His 243 triples rank fourth on the all-time major league list. Name him.

A Jake Beckley, who appeared in 2,377 games at first base, a big league record that stood until 1994, when Eddie Murray surpassed it. Beckley spent 20 years in the majors.

Q Did Roberto Clemente ever appear at a position other than the outfield?

A Yes. In 1956, his second season with the Pirates, Clemente played two games at second base and one at third.

Q Name the oldest Pirate to homer.

A Honus Wagner, who was 42 when he slugged the last of his 101 career home runs in 1916. Willie Stargell and pitcher Rip Sewell each homered at the age of 41.

Q Name the youngest player in Pirates history to homer.

A Bobby Del Greco, who slugged his first major league home run on June 9, 1952, just two months and two days after turning 19. Del Greco's solo shot off the Braves' Jim Wilson at Forbes Field wasn't enough to prevent a 3-2 Boston victory.

Dale Coogan (1950), Lee Walls (1952), Bill Mazeroski (1956) and Aramis Ramirez (1998), though older than Del Greco, were also 19 years of age when they first homered in a Pittsburgh uniform.

BIG MACK ATTACK

O nly once in his record 53 years as a major league manager was Connie Mack ejected from a game. The man remembered today as a kindly, mild-mannered sort—the very picture of serenity in the dugout—blew up on Sept. 6, 1895, while managing the Pirates in a game against New York at the Polo Grounds.

In fact, umpire Hank O'Day was compelled to summon several policemen to escort the recalcitrant Mack from the diamond after he used insulting and abusive language and questioned O'Day's integrity.

Mack snapped after New York's George Davis ripped a ball inside first leading off the fifth inning. Right fielder Patsy Donovan retrieved the ball and threw a strike to shortstop Frank Genins at second as Davis slid into the tag.

"Genins put the ball on Davis fully a yard from the bag. 'Safe,' said O'Day," noted the *Pittsburg Post*. "The Pirates were 'floored' with astonishment and even the spectators laughed. The decision was utterly ridiculous."

Mack and the Pirates, according to O.P. Caylor of the *New York Herald*, "exhausted their choicest rolling mill vituperation" in O'Day's honor. Mack was particularly savage, especially given that he and O'Day, a former pitcher, had often formed Washington's battery in the late 1880s.

"He began to hurl all sorts of epithets at O'Day, calling the latter a 'dirty robber' and names not quite so mild," wrote Caylor. "This he kept up for some time, until, at last, as O'Day asserts, Mack applied a name to him which is unprintable. It must have been something unusually provoking, for O'Day turned a gray-white in the face and, walking toward the bench, said, 'That will cost you $100.' "

O'Day also banished Mack from the grounds, although the latter "did not feel inclined to go," as *The New York Times* phrased it. Mack shook off a policeman called to "assist" his exit, at which point two more officers arrived. Realizing further resistance was futile, Mack left the premises without further delay.

Q In which decade did the Pirates achieve their greatest success, based on regular-season winning percentage?

A From 1900-09 the Bucs were 938-538, a .636 percentage. They also won four pennants and a World Series during that decade and finished second four times.

The 1920s rank second in terms of success (877-656, .572), followed by the 1970s (916-695, .569). Not surprisingly, the 1950s constitute the worst era in team history (616-923, .400).

Q How many teams have won more division championships than the Pirates?

A Only one. The Oakland Athletics have captured 10 titles since the divisional format was introduced in 1969. Pittsburgh and Atlanta rank second with nine championships apiece and Cincinnati, Los Angeles and Baltimore are tied for fourth with eight apiece.

Q Who were the Potato Bugs?

A That derisive nickname was stuck on the Pirates during the 1880s, when they wore uniforms that featured stripes, like a potato bug. Worse, the color scheme was blue and black.

Q What prompted Brooklyn manager Wilbert Robinson to declare, "They're beaten already," when describing the Pirates prior to Game 1 of the 1927 World Series?

A The Bucs watched, awestruck, as the Yankees bashed baseballs out of Forbes Field during batting practice. In those pre-television days, this was the National League champions' first look at the mighty New Yorkers and their famed "Murderers' Row" lineup. The effect was intimidating.

Even Pittsburgh's manager, Donie Bush, feared the Yankees' firepower. His last words to the Pirates, moments before Game 1, were "Let's go out on the ball field and hope we all don't get killed."

It's interesting to note that New York slugged only two home runs in its subsequent sweep of the Pirates, both by Babe Ruth.

Q Ruth slugged 60 home runs during the 1927 season to break his own single-season big league record. How many homers did the Pirates as a team hit that year?

A 54. Ruth's total exceeded that of 12 clubs. The Pirates' chief long-ball threats that season were shortstop Glenn Wright and right fielder Paul Waner, who hit nine apiece.

Q This Pirate holds a major league record that might well last an eternity—in 1912 he hit 36 triples. Name him.

A Owen "Chief" Wilson, who nearly doubled the total of his nearest challengers, teammate Honus Wagner and the Giants' Red Murray (20 each).

Wilson's record seems unassailable given that only three players since 1958 have so much as reached 20 triples—George Brett of the Royals in 1979 (with 20), teammate Willie Wilson in 1985 (21) and Lance Johnson of the Mets in 1996 (21).

Oddly enough, Chief Wilson never hit more than 14 triples in any of his eight other big league seasons.

Q Despite his record-setting season, Wilson doesn't even rank in the Pirates' career top 10 in triples. Who heads that list?

A Honus Wagner. He stroked 232 triples in his years with the Pirates and hit 252 all told, third-best all-time. Wilson finished with 94.

Q Which Pirates pitcher outscored and outrebounded 7-foot-1 Wilt Chamberlain of Kansas on the basketball court—even though he stood seven inches shorter?

A Oklahoma University's Don Schwall, who outscored Chamberlain 30-11 when the Big Eight Conference foes collided on Feb. 18, 1957. Schwall had earlier (Jan. 7) outrebounded his renowned adversary, 14-11.

In three showdowns with Chamberlain that season, Schwall won the scoring battle (73-69), but lost the war on the boards (46-31).

Schwall later spent three and a half seasons with the Pirates, coming to the club in 1963—the year Chamberlain won the fourth of his record seven consecutive NBA scoring crowns (a streak later matched by Michael Jordan).

Q Who holds the Pirates' record for consecutive games played?

A First baseman Gus Suhr, who participated in 822 consecutive games from Sept. 11, 1931, through June 4, 1937. Suhr's streak, which also set a National League record (broken 20 years later by Stan Musial), ended when he left the club for a few days due to his mother's death in San Francisco.

Suhr currently ranks ninth on the all-time major league list, behind Cal Ripken Jr. (2,632), Lou Gehrig (2,130), Everett Scott (1,307), Steve Garvey (1,207), Billy Williams (1,117), Joe Sewell (1,103), Musial (895) and Eddie Yost (829).

THE BENCHWARMER

I n an almost incomprehensible turn of events, manager Donie Bush benched future Hall of Famer Kiki Cuyler—a .309 hitter during the season—in the 1927 World Series.

The reason? They'd been feuding since midseason.

Cuyler first irritated Bush by questioning his decision to move him from third to second in the batting order, with rookie Lloyd Waner moving to third. Cuyler then found himself in Bush's doghouse when he didn't slide into second base to break up a double play during a game against New York (Cuyler explained he was trying to get hit by shortstop Travis Jackson's throw).

Bush also complained about Cuyler's high pegs from the outfield, which invariably enabled baserunners to advance. One day Bush confronted Cuyler and scolded him for missing the cut-off man. Cuyler replied that if Bush didn't like his throws, he could find somebody to take his place. Bush did just that. The first-year manager later told an acquaintance he was forced to punish Cuyler to maintain discipline.

Cuyler spent much of the season on the bench—he appeared in only 85 games after playing in every one the year before—and was not used at all in the Series. Bush's decision drew the wrath of the hometown fans, who booed him at every opportunity and continually chanted, "We want Cuyler." But Bush never relented.

"I was left on the bench to watch the Pirates lose four straight games to the Yankees, without getting a chance to stop the massacre," said Cuyler.

A month later he was traded to the Cubs.

Q This one-time Pirates catcher was behind the plate—as an umpire—for perhaps the most masterful pitching performance in big league history: Harvey Haddix's 12-inning perfect game in 1959. Name him.

A Vinnie Smith, who appeared in 16 games for the Bucs during the 1940s. A lack of power and a .259 batting average hastened Smith's retirement as a player, but he stayed in professional baseball by pursuing a career in umpiring. Smith worked National League games for nine seasons (1957-65).

Q First baseman Alex McKinnon went 4-for-4 to highlight the Pirates' 6-2 win in their National League debut on April 30, 1887. But despite that auspicious start, McKinnon's major league career was history nine weeks later. What happened?

A He died. The 30-year-old McKinnon was batting .340 when he took ill during a July 4 doubleheader in Philadelphia.

"One of the best players on the team has been overtaken by a serious illness," noted the *Pittsburgh Post*. "McKinnon was seized with a violent attack of cramps in the stomach and was compelled to go to bed."

He never recovered, succumbing to typhoid fever on July 24.

Q Who was the last active Pirate to die during the season?

A Pitcher Ernie "Tiny" Bonham, who succumbed on Sept. 15, 1949, due to complications resulting from an appendectomy. He was 36.

Bonham first complained of stomach pain during the Bucs' train trip from Chicago to St. Louis on Aug. 11. He pitched through the pain for several weeks—Bonham hurled a complete game victory over Philadelphia on Aug. 27 in his final appearance—before he was admitted to Presbyterian Hospital in Pittsburgh. Doctors performed an appendectomy on Sept. 8, but complications set in. Bonham's heart stopped during a second operation. He left a wife and two children.

"We are so terribly shocked over the tragic news that it would be impossible for any of us to express adequately the deep sorrow into which every one of us has been plunged," said Pirates assistant treasurer Al

Schlensker, acting as a team spokesman. "The heart of everyone in the organization is heavy with sadness."

Bonham compiled a 24-22 record in three seasons with Pittsburgh. He enjoyed his best years as a member of the New York Yankees, highlighted by a 21-5 season in 1942. Bonham led the American League in winning percentage (.808) and shutouts (6) and finished second in ERA (2.27) and victories. He appeared in three World Series as a Yankee and four-hit Brooklyn to win the deciding game of the 1941 Fall Classic.

What's ironic, given his untimely death, is that Bonham often quipped that he was unlucky and that the numbers were stacked against him. After all, Bonham pointed out, he was born in 1913, the 13th child in his family.

Q The Pirates retired Roberto Clemente's No. 21 in 1973, but that was not his original number with the Bucs. What was?

A 13.

Q Name the one-time Pirates coach who was swapped straight up for Norm Cash during his playing days in one of the most one-sided big league deals ever.

A Steve Demeter, a third baseman the Tigers traded to Cleveland on April 12, 1960, in exchange for Cash, who developed into an All-Star first baseman. Both players were 25 years of age.

Demeter never got another major league hit. Cash, on the other hand, won the American League batting crown (.361) in 1961, finished his career with 377 home runs and helped Detroit capture the 1968 World Series by hitting a torrid .385.

Demeter, a Homer City native, coached with the Bucs in 1985. He has served the organization for more than 25 years as a minor league manager, minor league batting instructor and scouting supervisor. He is currently employed as field coordinator of the minor league system.

Q This player made a name for himself before arriving in Pittsburgh, where he started on Frankie Frisch's 1944 and 1945 clubs. While with the Yankees, he replaced Lou Gehrig at first base, ending the Iron Horse's record streak of 2,130 consecutive games played. Name him.

A Babe Dahlgren, who started at first on May 2, 1939, when Gehrig asked manager Joe McCarthy if he could sit out that day's game at Detroit's Briggs Stadium. The future Hall of Famer, who'd been feeling sluggish, soon learned he was suffering from amyotrophic lateral sclerosis, which claimed his life two years later.

Dahlgren drove in a career-high 101 runs in 1944, batted .289 and clubbed a team-high 12 home runs, helping the Pirates to 90 wins and a second-place finish. That was Pittsburgh's best season since 1927, when Gehrig's Yankees thumped them in the World Series.

Q In what year did the Pirates win 93 games yet finish fourth?

A 1962. Despite a 93-68 record, Danny Murtaugh's club was scarcely a factor down the stretch. San Francisco and Los Angeles tied for first with 101 victories—the Giants captured the pennant in a riveting three-game playoff with their long-time rivals—and Cincinnati finished third with 98 wins.

The Bucs' .578 winning percentage in 1962 is the best ever by a fourth-place club in modern National League history.

Q The Pirates tied a major league standard at the outset of that 1962 season by winning their first 10 games. Which team ended their record run?

A Ironically enough, the worst club in the majors. The expansion New York Mets, who dropped their first nine games, pounded the unbeaten Bucs 9-1 at Forbes Field on April 23.

Exclaimed manager Casey Stengel afterward, "We sure was on a long nap. Someone must have given us a pill." Little did Stengel know that the Mets would slumber through much of the 1962 season and finish 40-120. Only one club in big league history—the 1899 Cleveland Spiders—lost more games (134).

Q The Bucs were involved in perhaps the most unusual rainout in major league history on June 15, 1976. Where?

A Indoors, at the Houston Astrodome. The game was postponed after a torrential downpour paralyzed the city. Ten inches of rain fell in seven hours, causing flash floods.

The players were already at the Astrodome when the storm struck, but umpires, fans and stadium personnel couldn't negotiate the flooded streets. The umps—Tom Gorman, Paul Pryor, Art Williams and John McSherry—tried to drive to the dome, but they wound up wading back to their hotel.

Some of the Astros were forced to spend the night in the clubhouse because their cars were submerged in the parking lot outside.

Conquering Alexander the Great

Pittsburgh's Emil Yde, a 24-year-old rookie, led the National League in winning percentage (.824, 16-3) and shutouts (4) in 1924. But on June 25, it was his hitting against a future Hall of Famer that turned heads and tamed the Cubs.

Yde smacked a three-run double with two outs in the ninth to erase a 6-3 deficit and then, after Chicago regained the lead in the 14th, rapped a two-run triple to give the Pirates an 8-7 victory. Both blows came off Grover Cleveland Alexander.

"Sounds like a Frank Merriwell story doesn't it? Yes, with young Emil Yde as the hero," wrote Ralph Davis in the *Pittsburgh Press*. "If ever a youngster won a place in the Pirate Hall of Fame, Mr. Yde did it yesterday."

Not only did Yde go 2-for-5 with five RBIs, he worked $10^1/_3$ solid innings of relief on the mound, relinquishing only one run and six hits.

The Cubs led 6-1 entering the bottom of the ninth at Forbes Field, but RBI singles by Charlie Grimm and Rabbit Maranville and Yde's bases-loaded double tied the score. Pittsburgh rallied again in the 14th after Chicago took a 7-6 lead. Clyde Barnhart doubled and Johnny Gooch drew a one-out walk.

"That brought Yde up in the second crisis," wrote H.L. Wollen of the *Press*. "Could he deliver again? He answered that question with a three-bagger to deep left, two runs went over and the greatest contest Pittsburgh fans had witnessed in many a day was over."

Why didn't manager Bill McKechnie pinch hit for his pitcher in either the ninth or 14th? It could be that McKechnie regarded Yde as the equal of any batsman he had left on the bench. Yde was certainly no slouch at the plate: He hit .239 that season and .233 for his career.

Q In which year did the Pirates last reach triple figures in victories?

A 1909. Fred Clarke's club won a franchise-record 110 games that season. The highest total any Pittsburgh team has reached since is 98 wins, in both 1979 and 1991.

Q Which Pirates regular posted the highest batting average in a given World Series?

A Second baseman Phil Garner, who hit .500 (12-for-24) against the Orioles in 1979. That also ranks as the team record for career World Series average (minimum 20 at bats).

Garner warmed up for the Fall Classic by batting .417 in the National League Championship Series vs. the Reds, giving him a torrid postseason figure of .472 (17-for-36). He hit a career-high .293 during the regular season.

Q Name the only Pirate to lead the league in saves following its recognition as an official statistic.

A Dave Giusti, who recorded 30 for the 1971 world champions. Elroy Face won three unofficial National League save titles, recording 20 in 1958, 17 in 1961 and 28 in 1962. It was Face's misfortune that saves were not granted official status until 1969, his final season in the majors.

Q Who holds the Pirates' single-season saves record?

A Jim Gott, with 34 in 1988.

Q How many different Pirates have led the league in triples?

A 21, a list that runs from Harry Davis in 1897 to Andy Van Slyke in 1988. Honus Wagner and Arky Vaughan each won three triples titles and Max Carey and Paul Waner claimed two apiece. The vast outfield expanses of Forbes Field and its predecessor, Exposition Park, practically invited a proliferation of three-base hits.

Q Which Pirates pitcher enjoyed one of his best seasons—17 victories— two years after he retired?

A Vernon Law, who called it quits because of shoulder trouble in 1963. He changed his mind and returned in 1964, finishing 12-13, and then went 17-9 with a 2.15 ERA—third-best in the National League—in 1965 to earn NL Comeback Player of the Year honors.
An ankle injury Law suffered in September of 1960 forced him to alter his delivery, which placed undue strain on his shoulder. By 1963, he was pitching in constant pain. Law's effectiveness—and, consequently, his workload—diminished.
"I was struggling," he recalled. "Finally, toward the end of the year, Danny Murtaugh came up to me. He tells me, 'Vern, if I was you, I'd retire. Don't just try to hang on.' I knew when he told me that that I wasn't gonna get an opportunity to pitch any more that year."

Law was 4-5 at the time with a 4.93 ERA in only 76²/₃ innings. He reluctantly announced his retirement and went back home to Idaho.

"But I kept working with the arm that winter," Law said. "Finally, the soreness began to leave. When it comes towards spring I give the Pirates a call—'If you want me, send me a contract.' So they decided to take a chance on me."

Their gamble paid huge dividends: Law won 29 games for Pittsburgh the next two seasons. Only Bob Veale (35) won more.

Q In what year did Mickey Mantle clear the right field roof of Forbes Field with a home run?

A No, it wasn't during the 1960 World Series. The Yankees slugger became only the third player in history to reach the roof when he connected off Bill Macdonald during an April 9, 1953, exhibition game against the Bucs.

Ironically, roof home runs were a topic of conversation earlier that day, when a Pittsburgh reporter asked Casey Stengel if he had been managing the Boston Braves when ex-Yankee Babe Ruth launched his 1935 shot over the grandstand (he wasn't). Another local reporter then asked Stengel if any of the current Yankees were capable of clearing the 86-foot roof.

"If anybody can do it, Mickey can," he replied. "He has a lot of power. You fellows don't get to see him much. Watch him today. He'll show you something."

Did he ever.

Q This Cincinnati pitcher debuted in spectacular fashion, firing a no-hitter against the Pirates in his first major league appearance. Name him.

A Charles "Bumpus" Jones, who closed out the 1892 season with a 7-1 win over Pittsburgh in the first no-hit game involving the Pirates. "The Pittsburgers were powerless in his hands," noted the *Pittsburg Press*.

Jones' no-hitter—the only one by a pitcher in his first game—was anything but a harbinger of big league success. He posted only one other victory in a major league career that came to an end in 1893—when Jones was 23 years of age.

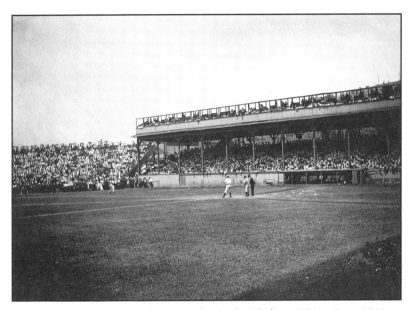

Exposition Park, the Pirates' home on the North Side from 1891 to June, 1909.

A concessionaire plies his wares from the second deck of Forbes Field. The view is down the third base line. Note the Carnegie Museum in the background.

Reunion of members of the first three Pirates championship teams: Tommy Leach (1900-12, 1918), Honus Wagner (1900-17), Claude Ritchey (1900-06), Kitty Bransfield (1901-04).

Paul Waner and Lloyd Waner, Big Poison and Little Poison.

The legendary Connie Mack donned umpires' garb for this photo with the legendary Honus Wagner. Mack managed the Pirates for 23 games in 1894 and all of the 1895 and 1896 seasons before moving on to a 50-year career in Philadelphia.

Pirates' manager Fred Clarke who ran the team from 1900-15. His team won National League pennants in 1901, 1902, 1903 and 1909. His 1909 club beat Ty Cobb and the Detroit Tigers four games to three to claim the World Series title.

Outfielder Max Carey (1910-26). Carey's .343 batting average in 1925 is the highest in a single season for a Pirates switch hitter. His total of 688 stolen bases is a team record.

Arkansas born shortstop Arky Vaughan (real name Joseph Floyd) played 1932-41. His .385 average in 1935 took the national league batting title and is the team record for highest average in a single season.

Outfielder Kiki Cuyler (real name Hazen Shirley) played for the Pirates 1921-27. He led the team in hitting in 1924 (.354) and 1925 (.357), but he sat out the 1927 World Series after a run-in with manager Donie Bush and was later traded.

Slugger Ralph Kiner crosses the plate and shakes the hand of teammate Wally Westlake. Kiner led the National League in home runs 1946-52.

Pirates' manager Danny Murtaugh (left) greets former manager Bill McKechnie during the 1960 World Series. Murtaugh had four different stints as the boss between 1957 and 1976. He led the Bucs to World Series titles in 1960 and 1971. McKechnie managed them from June 1922 through the end of the 1926 season, winning the World Series in 1925.

Manager Danny Murtaugh consoles pitcher Harvey Haddix, who lost his perfect game in the 13th inning in Milwaukee May 26, 1959.

Two broadcasting legends who brought Pirates' fans the games on radio. Rosey Rowswell (left) was behind the mike from 1936-1954. He was joined in 1948 by Bob Prince, who worked the radio booth for 28 years through 1975.

Shortstop Dick Groat, a Swissvale native, played for the Pirates in 1952 and 1955-62. Groat won the National College Basketball Player of the Year Award in 1951 as a guard at Duke University. He followed that by winning the National League MVP Award and National League batting title in 1960.

Bill Mazeroski in the field. He was arguably the finest fielding second baseman of all time. Note the 406 mark on the outfield wall at Forbes Field, which is where Mazeroski's home run to win the 1960 World Series left the park.

Mazeroski about to cross home plate after blasting the home run that sank the mighty Yankees.

Two icons of the post-World War II baby boomer generation, right fielder Roberto Clemente (left) and second baseman Bill Mazeroski. They were teammates on the 1960 and 1971 World Series championship teams.

A pitching coach's dream. Outstanding starting pitcher Vernon Law (left) and the baron of the bullpen, Elroy Face. They were teammates from 1955 through 1967.

Willie Stargell at the plate.

"Stargell takes it down the line." Affectionately known as "Pops", Stargell is the Pirates all-time home run leader and the hero of the 1979 World Series championship team.

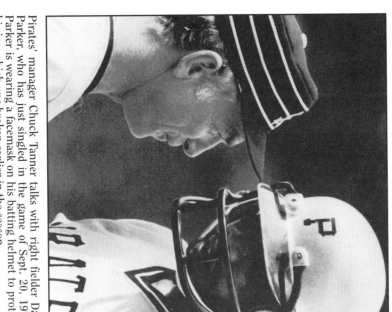

Pirates' manager Chuck Tanner talks with right fielder Dave Parker, who has just singled in the game of Sept. 20, 1978. Parker is wearing a facemask on his batting helmet to protect his jaw which was broken earlier in the season.

Jim Leyland, who managed the Pirates 1986-96. His teams won division titles in 1990, '91 and '92.

LOST IN A FOG

Fingers of fog rolled into Shea Stadium on the evening of May 25, 1979, lights produced an eerie glow and shadowy figures roamed the outfield.

Shea took on a ghostly appearance that night. In fact, Pirates left fielder Bill Robinson was nearly frightened to death.

In the 11th inning of a tie game, Joel Youngblood of the Mets lofted a routine fly ball to left that Robinson never saw. Fortunately, it landed 50 feet to his left—not on his head.

"I saw everyone pointing at me," said Robinson. "In a situation like that, all you can do is put up your hands."

And wish you'd worn a batting helmet into the field.

The umpires halted play at that point. When the soupy fog hadn't cleared following a wait of one hour, 18 minutes, they called the game. It went into the books as a 3-3 tie.

The fog first appeared during the middle innings and grew dense as the night wore on. Robinson told second base umpire Billy Williams that he couldn't see a thing as he trotted to his position in the bottom of the ninth.

Conditions worsened considerably by the time Youngblood led off the 11th with his fly to left. Robinson peered into the fog but failed to pick up the flight of the ball.

"See the ball in the air?" he said in response to a reporter's question. "I couldn't even see the pitcher throwing it to the batter."

Youngblood pulled into third with a triple. Manager Chuck Tanner stormed out of the dugout at that point and, along with several of his players, pleaded with the umpires to act. They stopped the game and, later, decided to call it.

"Fair enough," said Mets manager Joe Torre. "Youngblood would not have been on third if it hadn't been for the fog. This is an act of God and I'm not going to fool with that."

Q Only eight left-handers have caught in the major leagues since the turn of the century. The most recent was a Pirate. Name him.

A Benny Distefano, who appeared in three games behind the plate for the 1989 Bucs. He was a first baseman-outfielder by trade.

Because Distefano rarely stirred from the bench, he welcomed the opportunity to slip behind the plate in emergency situations and was frequently spotted warming up pitchers with his left-handed catcher's mitt, an unusual sight in the modern era. "I'll do anything to get a chance to play," he said.

Three of the other southpaw backstops spent time with the Pirates: first baseman Jiggs Donahue (1900-01 with the Bucs), who caught a total of 45 games with several teams; pitcher-first baseman Homer Hillebrand (1905-06, 1908), who appeared in three games behind the plate for the 1905 Pirates; and first baseman Dale Long (1951, 1955-57), who caught two games for the 1958 Cubs.

Q On April 13, 1963, Cincinnati's Pete Rose drilled his first major league hit—a triple—off which Pirates pitcher?

A Bob Friend. Rose, who was 0-for-11 before that extra-base blow at Forbes Field, would finish with a record 4,256 hits in his 24-year career.

Q This Hall of Fame manager led the Pirates to the National League title in 1925 and later guided the Cardinals (1928) and Reds (1939 and 1940) to the World Series. Name him.

A Bill McKechnie, who was born in the Pittsburgh suburb of Wilkinsburg. His 1925 and 1940 teams won world championships.
   McKechnie wasn't much of a player—he batted .251 with eight home runs in 11 major league seasons as an infielder, six of them spent in Pittsburgh—but he had few peers as a manager. In fact, McKechnie and Dick Williams (1967 Red Sox, 1972-73 Athletics, 1984 Padres) are the only managers to win pennants with three different teams.
   The Pirates' spring training stadium in Bradenton, Fla., is named for McKechnie, a 1962 Hall of Fame inductee.

Q Which Pirates broadcaster won a $20 bet with first baseman Dick Stuart by diving from his third-floor room into St. Louis' Chase Hotel swimming pool?

A The flamboyant Bob Prince, who once boasted, "I'll do anything for 20 bucks." Prince backed up his boast with a daring dive in 1959.
   "I had to clear eight feet of sidewalk," he said. "What I didn't tell him was that I was a varsity diver in college." Prince also participated in swimming events at Pitt in the 1930s.
   "The pool was adjacent to the hotel," recalled Prince's former broadcast partner, Nellie King. "It's a helluva dangerous jump, but he knew he could do it. It was kind of a crazy thing to do, I guess."
   Recalling his wager and subsequent leap years later, Prince offered only one regret: Stuart never did pay up.

Q This one-time Pirates employee still holds a dubious American League catching record. On June 28, 1907, the Washington Senators successfully stole 13 bases against him en route to a 16-5 victory. Name him.

A Branch Rickey, who served as the Pirates' general manager from 1951 to 1956.

Rickey was a member of the New York Highlanders when Washington repeatedly tested his arm—and repeatedly found it wanting. A headline in *The New York Times* underscored his plight: "Diminutive catcher of the New Yorks fails to stop runners of the Senatorial outfit." Rickey also committed an error, one of 31 he made in 120 career games.

Q Which Pirate missed a bunt sign during the 1971 World Series and promptly smacked a three-run homer to clinch a Game 3 victory?

A First baseman Bob Robertson, who batted against Mike Cuellar in the seventh inning with the Bucs clinging to a 2-1 lead. When Roberto Clemente and Willie Stargell reached base to open the inning, third base coach Frank Oceak relayed manager Danny Murtaugh's bunt sign to Robertson.

He missed the sign but not the pitch, which wound up in the right-center field stands, sealing a 5-1 victory. Said Stargell to Robertson as his teammate arrived at home plate, "Attaway to bunt that ball."

Q This Pirate holds the distinction of being the only pitcher to win three games in a World Series his team lost. Name him.

A Deacon Phillippe, who accounted for all the Pittsburgh victories in 1903, when the Red Sox captured the inaugural Series five games to three. Phillippe won Games 1, 2 and 4 before losing Games 7 and 8. Incredibly, he completed all five of his starts.

Team owner Barney Dreyfuss rewarded Phillippe with a bonus and 10 shares of stock in the Pirates for his heroic efforts.

Q Name the last Pirate to slug three home runs in a single game.

A Third baseman Darnell Coles, who homered twice off the Cubs' Jamie Moyer and once off Drew Hall on Sept. 30, 1987, to equal the team record during a 10-8 loss to Chicago. Coles had hit only two home runs in 102 previous at bats for the Pirates that year.

Q This player didn't make much of an impression as a Pirates catcher in the 1950s, but his impact was unmistakable as the club's general manager years later. He acquired Bill Madlock, Phil Garner, Bert Blyleven and Tim Foli in deals that helped bring a world championship to Pittsburgh in 1979. Name him.

A Harding Peterson, who served as the Bucs' general manager from 1976 to 1985. Peterson appeared in only 66 games as a backup catcher during a four-season span in Pittsburgh. He batted .273 with three home runs.

ALL FOR NAUGHT

Poor Harry McIntire. The Brooklyn pitcher no-hit Pittsburgh for 10²/₃ innings on Aug. 1, 1906—the longest no-hitter in major league history apart from Harvey Haddix's 1959 gem—yet he didn't even earn a victory for his efforts. Like Haddix, McIntire wound up an undeserving loser.

The 27-year-old right-hander was untouchable for 10 innings at Washington Park, keeping the Pittsburgh batters completely off balance.

"McIntyre [sic] was in wonderful shape and he had the Pirates guessing all the way," noted an account in the *Pittsburg Press*. "Inning after inning was reeled off without the Pirates seeing first. McIntyre worked so cleverly that for 10 long innings not a single hit was made off his delivery, only 31 men facing him in all that time."

Unfortunately for McIntire, his pitching counterpart, Lefty Leifield, was just as effective in keeping Brooklyn off the scoreboard, sending the masterpiece into extra innings.

Second baseman Claude Ritchey finally broke up McIntire's gem with a single to left field in the 11th inning. But the real heartbreak came in the 13th. Bob Ganley led off with a single, raced to third on Honus Wagner's double and scored on Jim Nealon's single. Leifield then retired the Dodgers in the bottom half of the 13th for a 1-0 victory.

Despite yielding only four hits and a walk in 13 innings, McIntire went home a loser.

Q While Bill Mazeroski is arguably the greatest defensive second baseman in major league history, he does not hold the Pirates' single-season record for fielding percentage at his position. Who does?

A Johnny Ray, whose .993 percentage in 1986 beat the mark of .992 Maz set 20 years before. Ray committed only five errors in 151 games.

Q Two players who later managed the Pirates each homered in their first major league at bat. Name them.

A Chuck Tanner and Gene Lamont. Neither one slugged too many more after debuting with a such a bang.

Tanner, who managed the Bucs for nine seasons (1977-85), connected on the first pitch he saw from Cincinnati's Gerry Staley on April 12, 1955. "It was the thrill of my life," said Tanner, a Milwaukee Braves outfielder. "I pinch hit for [pitcher] Warren Spahn, who was a pretty good hitter." In fact, Spahn finished his major league career with more home runs (35) than Tanner (21).

Lamont, who was selected before future Hall of Famer Johnny Bench in the 1965 draft, slugged only four home runs in five seasons as a Detroit catcher. He hit the first off Boston's Cal Koonce on Sept. 2, 1970. Lamont served as a Pittsburgh coach for seven seasons (1986-91, 1996) before succeeding Jim Leyland as the Bucs' manager in 1997.

Q Which Pirate once slugged a batting practice home run into a tuba?

A Willie Stargell, whose shot over the center field fence at Minnesota's Metropolitan Stadium prior to the 1965 All-Star game scattered members of a band preparing for the pre-game ceremonies. A tuba player, unfortunately, didn't react swiftly enough: The baseball plunked directly into the opening of the instrument.

Stargell later cleared the fence in the game, hitting a two-run homer off the Twins' Mudcat Grant that helped the National League post a 6-5 victory. Oddly enough, that was the only All-Star game home run of his career.

Q Which Pirates manager won the highest percentage of games during his tenure with the team (minimum 100 games)?

A Fred Clarke, who led the Bucs to a 1,422-969 record (.595) between 1900 and 1915. Next in line is Bill McKechnie (.583 from 1922 to 1926), followed by Donie Bush (.580 from 1927 to 1929), Al Buckenberger (.565 from 1892 to 1894) and Bill Virdon (.560 in 1972 and 1973).

Hall of Famer Joe McCarthy is the major league record holder for winning percentage (minimum of 1,000 games) with a .615 figure. McCarthy directed the Yankees to six world titles between 1936 and 1943.

Q In what year did the Pirates nearly go on strike?

A 1946. Attorney Robert Murphy's goal was to organize major leaguers into the American Baseball Guild, which advocated free agency and salary arbitration long before such concepts became reality.

Murphy focused on the Pirates in his recruiting efforts and signed 23 of the 25 players. "Pittsburgh is the testing block, the guinea pig for the entire Guild movement," wrote Chet Smith in the *Pittsburgh Press.*

On June 7, Murphy met with the team in the Forbes Field clubhouse and asked the players to not take the field that night. Only after an impassioned plea by pitcher Rip Sewell—one of the non-ABG members—did the Pirates vote to play.

The Bucs beat New York 10-5, after which the Guild movement gradually lost momentum.

Q Which Pirate owns the distinction of being the oldest player in the 20th century to hit an inside-the-park home run?

A Honus Wagner, who was 42 years, four months and seven days old on July 1, 1916, when he circled the bases in a 2-1 victory at Cincinnati's Crosley Field. The day was brutally hot, which took a toll on the Bucs' senior member.

"Wagner was in bad shape when he reached the Pirate bench after making his wild dash around the bases," noted Chilly Doyle of the *Pittsburgh Post-Gazette.* "Anxious hands were waiting to swing the towels over that venerable brow as Honus staggered to the dugout."

Washington's Jim O'Rourke set the all-time record with an inside-the-park home run on June 9, 1893, against Cleveland. He was 42 years, nine months and eight days old.

Q What was notable—and historic—about the Pirates' 10-7 victory over Philadelphia at Three Rivers Stadium on Sept. 1, 1971?

A For the first time in major league history, a team started an all-black lineup: catcher Manny Sanguillen, first baseman Al Oliver, second baseman Rennie Stennett, shortstop Jackie Hernandez, third baseman Dave Cash, left fielder Willie Stargell, center fielder Gene Clines, right fielder Roberto Clemente and pitcher Dock Ellis.

Some of the players did not immediately grasp the significance of the moment.

"About the third or fourth inning Dave Cash says to me, 'Scoop, we've got all brothers out here,' " Oliver recalled. "I look around and I said, 'We sure do.' "

There was speculation that manager Danny Murtaugh started Oliver—who rarely played against left-handed pitchers—in place of Bob Robertson just to complete an all-black lineup. But Murtaugh himself shot down that theory.

"I put the nine best athletes out there," Murtaugh explained in the post-game interview. "The best nine I put out there tonight happened to be black. No big deal. Next question."

Q Ralph Kiner won or shared a record seven consecutive National League home run crowns. How many times did Kiner lead the NL in strikeouts?

A Just once, with 109 in his rookie year of 1946. Kiner never exceeded 100 again.

Q Nearly a century after last pitching for the Pirates, this left-hander still ranks as the franchise's career leader in winning percentage. Name him.

A Jesse Tannehill, who compiled a 116-58 (.667) record from 1897 through 1902. He won 20 games or more four times during his six seasons in Pittsburgh.

Tannehill posted 25 and 24 victories, respectively, in 1898 and 1899 and was 20-6 in both 1900 and 1902. He led the league with a 2.18 ERA in 1901, then improved to a career-best 1.95 a year later, although he finished only third in the NL.

No Surrender

P irates manager Jim Leyland cried as he recounted the events of April 21, 1991. Actually, it was the Chicago Cubs who should have been shedding tears.

They led 7-2 after seven and a half innings, only to watch the Bucs rally to tie the score with two outs in the ninth. The Cubs regrouped and grabbed another five-run lead in the 11th. Unfazed, the Pirates erupted for six runs in the bottom half of the inning to complete the greatest extra-inning comeback in major league history and secure a riveting 13-12 victory. Paul Meyer of the *Pittsburgh Post-Gazette* called it "The North Side Miracle."

"I've never seen a game like that, even in my son's Little League," said Pirates pitcher Neal Heaton. "I've never seen anything like that. Unbelievable."

Tears welled in Leyland's eyes as he described how his team not once, but twice, erased five-run deficits.

"That was the greatest game I've ever been part of," he said. "These guys come in here every day and bust their butts. They don't give up. They don't quit."

Pittsburgh drew within striking distance by plating four runs in the eighth, the key blows a two-run triple by Orlando Merced and Bobby Bonilla's two-run homer. Pinch hitter Gary Varsho, who had been traded by the Cubs to the Pirates earlier in the month, then delivered an RBI double off closer Lee Smith to tie the game in the ninth.

Chicago seemingly put the game on ice in the 11th when Andre Dawson followed Doug Dascenzo's tie-breaking RBI single with a grand slam. But the Bucs refused to throw in the towel.

Jose Lind drew a leadoff walk against Heathcliff Slocumb and Curtis Wilkerson and Merced followed with singles to load the bases and chase Slocumb. Jay Bell greeted former Pirate Mike Bielecki with a two-run double and Andy Van Slyke hit a sacrifice fly to slice the deficit to 12-10.

After Bonilla drew a base on balls and Bonds knocked in a run with a single, Gary Redus walked to load the bases for Don Slaught, who was still seething over a missed opportunity: He had bounced out to end the 10th with the potential winning run at third base. This time Slaught did not fail, drilling a double over center fielder Jerome Walton's head as Bonilla and Bonds gleefully raced home with the tying and winning runs.

"That was unbelievable," said Slaught of the six-run uprising. "That would be hard to do against batting practice pitching. It was like the last team that batted would win."

Few teams wipe out five-run deficits twice in one game. None had ever wiped out a five-run deficit in extra innings.

"It was weird," said Bonds. "The weirdest game I've ever been in."

Q A 1986 game between the Pirates and Padres at San Diego's Jack Murphy Stadium was delayed six minutes for what unusual reason?

A A skunk waddled onto the diamond in the top of the seventh inning, scattering San Diego's fielders. The intruder strolled from beneath the stands behind first base and headed for the infield as 20,515 fans dissolved in hysterical laughter.

The grounds crew finally shooed the skunk under the left field stands and play resumed. "It raised a ruckus, but luckily not its tail," cracked Bob Hertzel of the *Pittsburgh Press*.

Q In what year did the Pirates play their first Sunday game in Pittsburgh?

A 1934. The Bucs defeated Cincinnati 9-5 on April 29.

Until Pennsylvania repealed its so-called Blue Laws, professional sports were among the activities banned on Sundays. Across the state in Philadelphia, the Phillies also played their inaugural Sunday home game that April 29, losing 8-7 to Brooklyn.

Q Roberto Clemente and Bill Mazeroski were members of the Pirates' 1960 world championship team and the Bucs' first National League East title club 10 years later. Name the only other individual who played for both teams.

A Pitcher Joe Gibbon, who had been traded away following the 1965 season before returning to Pittsburgh in 1969. Danny Murtaugh managed both championship clubs.

Q The Pirates were the first major league team to wear double-knit uniforms. What year?

A 1970. The Bucs donned their new duds for the inaugural game at Three Rivers Stadium on July 16, 1970, against Cincinnati. The mod look did not elicit universal approval.

"The Pirates' new uniforms looked like the designer had crossed a softball outfit with a pair of Carol Burnett's old pajamas," wrote Phil Musick in the *Pittsburgh Press*.

Nevertheless, the style caught on. Within two years, nearly every big league team was clad in double knits.

Q What was the name of the fenced enclosure erected in front of the Forbes Field scoreboard prior to the 1947 season?

A Greenberg Gardens, which one critic described as a "barbed-wire eyesore." The Gardens stretched from the left field foul pole to left-center field and housed both bullpens.

The enclosure reduced the distance down the left field line by 30 feet to a more reasonable 335, an important consideration given the team's offseason acquisition of four-time American League home run champion Hank Greenberg from Detroit. The Pirates hoped a more inviting target would boost his home run production.

When Greenberg retired following the season, the "eyesore" was renamed Kiner's Korner in honor of home run champion Ralph Kiner. The enclosure was removed following the 1953 season, after Kiner was dealt to the Cubs.

Q In its 61-year history, no pitcher ever threw a no-hitter at Forbes Field. Who came closest?

A Jeff Tesreau of the New York Giants. Tesreau baffled the Bucs for eight and two-thirds innings on May 16, 1914, before the slumping Joe Kelly—"who hadn't made a hit since Rome fell," according to the *Pittsburgh Press*—lined a single to center.

"There wasn't a flaw or taint to Kelly's single in the ninth," noted James Jerpe of the *Pittsburgh Gazette Times*. "It was clean as a whistle over second base."

The only other Pirates baserunner was Jimmie Viox, who drew a one-out walk in the eighth. Tesreau finished with a one-hit 2-0 victory, one of his 26 wins that season.

Q Which Pirate came closest to breaking Forbes Field's no-hit jinx?

A Bob Moose, who was making only his fifth career start when he held the Houston Astros hitless for seven and two-thirds innings on June 14, 1968.

Julio Gotay, an ex-Pirate, spoiled Moose's masterpiece with a bloop single to right center. The 20-year-old rookie finished with a two-hit 3-0 victory.

Moose did enter his name on the no-hit honor roll the following season against the pennant-bound Mets at Shea Stadium.

Q Who holds the Pirates' record for RBIs in a season?

A Not Ralph Kiner, not Willie Stargell, not a power hitter at all, really. In 1927—a year in which he hit but nine homers—Paul Waner knocked in 131 runs to lead the National League.

Kiner does rank second, with 127 RBIs in both the 1947 and 1949 seasons. Stargell's career best was 125 in 1971.

Q Which pitcher holds the Pirates' record for postseason wins?

A Bruce Kison, with four. Kison was 3-0 in National League Championship Series play and 1-1 in the World Series. Steve Blass, Deacon Phillippe and Babe Adams share runner-up honors with three victories apiece.

Incidentally, Kison won an American League Championship Series game with California in 1982 to finish his career with a 5-1 postseason mark.

WATERLOGGED WINS

P ittsburgh's doubleheader sweep of Brooklyn on July 4, 1902, was a high-water mark for the reigning National League champs—quite literally. The Pirates' 3-0 and 4-0 victories that day were achieved against perhaps the most unusual backdrop in major league history.

Much of Exposition Park, which was located on the banks of the Allegheny River, was underwater. Heavy rains had caused the Allegheny to overflow its banks, which left the outfield submerged in spots.

By the second half of the morning-afternoon twinbill, outfielders actually waded to their positions. A headline in the *Pittsburg Post* read, "Grounds are flooded and outfielders indulge in swimming and diving feats." That was only a slight exaggeration.

"When the people entered the grounds, nothing of a flood was visible," noted the *Post* account. "By and by, water was seen to glisten between the blades of grass in right center field. By degrees the water rose and formed pools.

"Little islands were scattered among them and on these the center and right fielders took refuge. They were chased off these islands by the incoming flood, and by the end of the game a smooth body of treacherous-looking water lay in center and right fields and lapped the new bleachers."

The presence of this outfield "lake" necessitated a special ground rule, instituted for only that day, declaring that any ball hit into the water was a single. Noted the *Pittsburg Press*, "by afternoon the outfielders were nearly knee deep in water, and the way they played in spite of this handicap was a source of pleasure to the crowd."

Pirates officials would have canceled the doubleheader under normal circumstances, but a large holiday turnout was expected (more than 20,000 fans attended) because Pittsburgh was leading the league and the Dodgers were lodged in second place.

Incidentally, Brooklyn's second baseman in both games sported an appropriate name given the circumstances: Tim Flood.

Q Which Pirate won the National League batting title by raising his average a whopping 111 points from the year before?

A Outfielder Matty Alou, who batted .231 with the 1965 Giants before a trade brought him to Pittsburgh—and to manager Harry Walker, who served as his personal tutor. Walker encouraged Alou to abandon his pull-hitting style and become a spray hitter.

"Then I told him to get a bigger bat—a heavier bat," Walker recalled. "He used to swing that little bat and he had a buggy-whip swing. With a bigger, thicker-handled bat, he could wait longer. He had better bat control."

The change paid immediate dividends: Alou boosted his average to a major league-best .342 in 1966.

"That winter after I was traded by the Giants, [new teammate and fellow Dominican] Manny Mota told me that Harry Walker knew a lot about hitting," Alou recalled. "I listened to Harry when I first got to camp. I figured, what did I have to lose? When you hit only .231, you had better listen to someone."

Ironically, Alou's turnaround paralleled Walker's two decades before: He went from a .237 hitter in 1946 to an NL batting champion (.363) a year later.

Only one batting champ in big league history made a more dramatic jump from the previous season (minimum 300 at bats) than Walker: Colorado's Andres Galarraga, who hit .370 in 1993 after slumping to .243 with the Cardinals a year earlier.

Q Which Pirates coach was a teammate of both Hank Aaron and Sadaharu Oh, the two most prolific home run hitters in professional baseball history?

A Current third base coach Jack Lind, an infielder with the Milwaukee Brewers when Aaron was wrapping up his career in 1975. Two years later Lind concluded his own pro career with the Yomiuri Giants of the Japanese Central League, whose featured performer was Oh. The Giants first baseman slugged 868 career homers to Aaron's 755.

"They were two different people," said Lind. "Aaron had big hands and tremendous innate power. Oh was smaller in stature. He depended on strict, disciplined hitting mechanics."

Only one other individual was a teammate of both Aaron and Oh: second baseman Davey Johnson, now manager of the Los Angeles Dodgers.

"My career was very undistinguished," said Lind, who appeared in 26 games for the Brewers in 1974 and 1975. "But there are only two of us who played with both of them. That's kind of special."

Q This Pirate ranks as one of the finest control pitchers of all time. He led the National League in fewest walks per nine innings four consecutive seasons and finished second in that category three times. Name him.

A Babe Adams, who gave up the fewest walks per nine innings from 1919 through 1922. He still holds major league records for the fewest walks issued, 250 or more innings (19 in 263 innings in 1920) and for pitching the longest game without walking a batter (his 21-inning masterpiece against New York in 1914).

Adams allowed only 1.29 walks per nine innings during his career, the second-best figure in baseball history since 1893, when the distance between the mound and home plate was increased from 50 feet to 60 feet, six inches. Only Deacon Phillippe—Adams' teammate for parts of four seasons—posted a better average: 1.25.

Q How many Pirates have won the Rookie of the Year award, which was inaugurated by the Baseball Writers Association of America in 1947?

A None. Of course, Johnny Ray (1982) and Jason Kendall (1996) were selected as the National League Rookie of the Year by *The Sporting News*. The BBWAA opted for a pair of Dodgers, Steve Sax and Todd Hollandsworth, those years.

It should also be noted that three Pirates—Don Robinson (1978), Mike Dunne (1987) and Tim Wakefield (1992)—have earned Rookie Pitcher of the Year honors from *The Sporting News*.

Q In what year did the Pirates win 98 games—and *not* win a title of any sort?

A 1908. Pittsburgh tied the New York Giants for second place, one game behind the champion Cubs.

The Bucs gained their revenge a year later: Chicago won 104 games yet failed to beat out the Bucs, who posted 110 victories. The Cubs thus established a record for wins in a pennantless season.

Brooklyn tied the mark in 1942 and the Atlanta Braves eclipsed it in 1998 with 106 victories. The Braves were denied a pennant when San Diego bumped them off in the National League Championship Series.

Q Who was Sister Sledge?

A A musical group whose hit song, *We Are Family*, was adopted by the 1979 Pirates as their anthem. The close-knit Bucs, who likened themselves to a family, went on to win the world championship.

"We didn't mean to be sassy or fancy, but we felt the song typified our ball club," said first baseman Willie Stargell. "We loved each other."

Thus the team's apt association with the song.

Q This fixture's career as a Pirates employee spanned nine decades, a length of service unmatched in team history. Name him.

A Art McKennan, best known as the Bucs' long-time public address announcer.

McKennan began working for the Pirates in 1919 at the age of 12 as an errand boy for the players. He became a bat boy the following year and later worked as an usher. McKennan was the Bucs' full-time PA announcer from 1948 to 1986 and called games on a part-time basis until bowing out on April 11, 1993, at the age of 86.

Q Jim Leyland once managed which future Pittsburgh Steelers starter?

A Quarterback Bubby Brister, a Steeler from 1986 to 1992 and a starter for three seasons. Before signing an NFL contract, Brister gave professional baseball a whirl. He spent the fall of 1981 playing for the Tigers' Dunedin club in the Florida Instructional League, managed by Leyland.

Brister played shortstop and outfield that summer with Bristol (Va.) of the Appalachian Rookie League after Detroit selected him in the fourth round of the amateur draft. A .180 batting average and 27 strikeouts in 39 games—not to mention an .864 fielding percentage—clearly indicated he was not a big league prospect. At least not in baseball.

Brister is currently with the Denver Broncos.

Q Which member of the 1960 Pirates signed his first professional contract after climbing out of a swimming hole and, soaking wet, throwing a few pitches?

A Wilmer "Vinegar Bend" Mizell, who signed with the Cardinals after showing his stuff to a team scout during an unorthodox audition in his Alabama hometown of Vinegar Bend (hence the nickname).

A FAN-TASTIC PERFORMANCE

J ohn Candelaria, a 21-year-old rookie, seemed overmatched as he stepped onto the mound for Game 3 of the 1975 National League Championship Series against the vaunted Cincinnati Reds.

Instead, it was the Reds who were overmatched.

Candelaria tied an LCS record by striking out 14 batters in seven and two-thirds innings at Three Rivers Stadium on the evening of Oct. 7 and did all he could to help the Pirates stave off elimination. But it wasn't enough.

Pete Rose drilled a two-out, two-run homer in the eighth inning to put Cincinnati ahead 3-2 and knock the rookie from the mound. The Reds then pushed across a run in the 10th to win 4-3, sweep the best-of-five series and spoil Candelaria's heroics. Said an admiring Rose, "It might have been the greatest pressure game I've seen any pitcher pitch."

Unfortunately, it was all for naught.

"At the time I felt pretty bad about the way the game went," said Candelaria. "But now when I think about it, it seems like I did a pretty good job for a kid, a 21-year-old rookie. It was one of the best games I ever pitched. It's something I'll never forget."

Candelaria's strikeout record stood until Oct. 11, 1997, when Mike Mussina of Baltimore fanned 15 batters against Cleveland in the ALCS. Mussina held sole possession of the standard for all of 24 hours: Florida rookie Livan Hernandez struck out 15 in an NLCS victory over Atlanta the very next day.

Q The major leagues' first night game was played on May 24, 1935, at Cincinnati's Crosley Field. How many years passed before the Pirates hosted a game under the lights?

A Five. The Bucs walloped Boston 14-2 at Forbes Field on June 4, 1940. By then, eight other teams had introduced night baseball at their ballparks.

A crowd of 20,319 filed into Forbes Field for the historic game, which didn't start until 9:28 p.m. because the clubs waited for total darkness. Workers needed four months to install the lights—or as much time as it required to build the entire ballpark in 1909.

Q The Pirates' winning pitcher in that game, Joe Bowman, also played a role in the *majors'* first night game. What was it?

A Pitching for the Phillies, Bowman was saddled with the loss as the Reds emerged with a 2-1 victory.

Q In what country was Honus Wagner—dubbed "The Flying Dutchman"—born?

A Trick question. Wagner was born in the Allegheny County community of Chartiers, which merged with Mansfield in 1894 to form Carnegie, named for Pittsburgh steel magnate Andrew Carnegie. Wagner's birthplace is located about five miles southwest of Pittsburgh.

Q This Pirates hurler served up his so-called "eephus" pitch—a bloop delivery—to Ted Williams in the 1946 All-Star game. The Red Sox slugger smashed the offering into the Fenway Park bullpen for a three-run homer, capping a 4-for-4 afternoon that featured two home runs and a record five RBIs. Who threw the eephus?

A Rip Sewell, who won 143 games in 12 seasons with the Bucs. He developed the unusual pitch because a leg injury limited his effectiveness with more conventional deliveries.

Sewell first used the high-arc eephus against rookie outfielder Dick Wakefield during a 1942 spring training game against Detroit.

"Wakefield started to swing, then he stopped, then he swung again," Sewell recalled. "He almost fell down when he missed."

Sewell expressed no regrets in trying to fool Williams with the eephus in the All-Star game.

"I figured I had nothing to lose," he said. "Williams was hitting everything else that came within reach."

Q How did Sewell suffer his injury?

A He was walking through tall reeds while hunting in Florida in December of 1941 when another hunter mistook him for game and fired his shotgun. Numerous pellets lodged in Sewell's legs; some were removed, some remained.

Sewell rebounded in 1942 to win a team-high 17 games. Only seven big league pitchers exceeded that total.

Noted Edward F. Balinger in the *Pittsburgh Post-Gazette*, "The veteran moundsman made such a narrow escape from death that it was regarded as remarkable that he recovered sufficently to come back and climb among the topnotchers in the major leagues."

Ironically, Sewell posted a better winning percentage after the accident (.613, 103-65) than before (.556, 40-32).

Q What was the "Immaculate Deflection"?

A A poor cousin to the storied "Immaculate Reception," which also took place at Three Rivers Stadium. The fortuitous deflection enabled the Pirates to win the 1974 National League East title on the final day of the season.

The Bucs trailed Chicago 4-3 with two outs in the ninth when pinch hitter Bob Robertson struck out swinging at Rick Reuschel's 3-2 pitch to apparently end the game. But the ball eluded catcher Steve Swisher, who compounded his misfortune by hurrying his peg to first in an effort to retire the lumbering Robertson. The ball glanced off Robertson's shoulder, enabling Manny Sanguillen to score the tying run.

"That might be the most important strikeout of my life," said Robertson. In what was surely a Pittsburgh first, the fans actually gave Robertson a standing ovation for whiffing when he departed for a pinch runner moments later. The Pirates scored a run in the 10th to win the game—and the division crown—by a 5-4 score.

Two years before, the Pittsburgh Steelers pulled out an improbable come-from-behind victory when Franco Harris caught a deflected Terry Bradshaw pass in the final seconds and ran for a touchdown to beat the Oakland Raiders in the AFC playoffs. That play, which sealed the first postseason victory in Steelers history, came to be known as the "Immaculate Reception."

Q This Pirates pitcher first gained attention in Pittsburgh as a catcher— of footballs. He caught 91 passes as a Pitt tight end in the late 1960s. Name him.

A George Medich, who also punted for the Panthers. Medich played three years of football at Pitt (1967-69). He returned to Pittsburgh in 1976 as a member of the Pirates' starting rotation.

Q Which Pirates manager once led the National League in steals—with the modest total of 18—during his playing days?

A Danny Murtaugh, who won the title in 1941 as a rookie second baseman with Philadelphia. No NL leader since has finished with a lower total. Murtaugh later played for the Bucs (1948-51).

Q Name the only Pirate to end an All-Star game with a winning hit.

A Roberto Clemente, whose 10th-inning single in the first of two games in 1961 scored Willie Mays from second, giving the National League a come-from-behind 5-4 victory at Candlestick Park. Mays had doubled home Hank Aaron moments earlier, erasing a 4-3 deficit.

Before Clemente, only two players had ended All-Star games with a hit: Ted Williams crashed a dramatic three-run homer with two outs in the ninth to give the American League a 7-5 victory in 1941 and Stan Musial socked a 12th-inning solo homer to lift the National League to a 6-5 win in 1955.

REVENGE OF THE LITTLE LEAGUERS

I t was only one victory in an 80-82 season, but there was undeniably something special about the Pirates' 8-2 win at New York on Sept. 26, 1987.

"I wanted that game as much as I've ever wanted a game," said manager Jim Leyland.

The reason? Mets pitcher Dwight Gooden, who opened a veritable Pandora's box by opening his mouth. Gooden dismissed the Bucs as a bunch of Little Leaguers after they took two of three from the Mets the previous weekend at Three Rivers Stadium.

"I don't like them. They're too cocky," he told Bob Klapisch of the *New York Post*. "I saw a lot of Little League stuff [in Pittsburgh]—high-fiving, jumping around . . . it was like watching the Little League World Series. I could see if they were headed for the playoffs or something. But they're a fifth-place team. I wouldn't be acting like that if I was on a fifth-place team."

Gooden, who was 7-0 lifetime against Pittsburgh, then guaranteed win No. 8.

Trainer Kent Biggerstaff clipped the story, underlined the offending quote and taped it to a cooler in the Pirates clubhouse. The article didn't go unnoticed.

The Bucs sent a message to Gooden when they next faced him, without uttering a word. They spoke with their bats, scoring five quick runs and knocking New York's ace from the box after three innings en route to an 8-2 victory.

Gooden's aura of invincibility against the Pirates was shattered that day. He has since compiled a 5-12 record against Pittsburgh.

Q Name the last Pirates rookie to lead the team in home runs.

A Outfielder Al Martin, who hit 18 in 1993. In fact, two other rookies—second baseman Carlos Garcia and outfielder Dave Clark—finished second and third with 12 and 11 homers, respectively.

Q Name the last rookie pitcher to lead the Pirates in wins.

A Mike Dunne, who posted 13 victories in 1987. Dunne finished with a 13-6 record and ranked second in the league in earned run average (3.03). He went 12-24 with a 4.63 ERA the rest of his career.

Q Name the last rookie to lead the Pirates in batting.

A Catcher Jason Kendall, who hit .300 in 1996. Al Martin also hit .300 to share team honors.

Not since outfielder Richie Zisk hit .324 in 1973 had a rookie paced the Pirates in batting (minimum 300 at bats).

Q Which Pirate once slammed 11 home runs in 12 games against a single opponent one season?

A Willie Stargell, who bombarded the Braves in 1971, hitting six homers at Three Rivers Stadium and five in Atlanta. He struck three times against the Braves at Atlanta-Fulton County Stadium on April 10 and slammed three more off Braves pitching 11 days later in Pittsburgh.

Stargell, Harmon Killebrew (1969) and Dale Murphy (1983) share the single-season major league record for most homers against one opponent in a 12-club league. The all-time mark of 14 was set by Lou Gehrig against Cleveland in 1936, back when teams faced one another 22 times each year.

Q The Pirates' batting practice pitcher during their world championship year of 1960 is one of only five pitchers in major league history to throw two no-hitters in a single season. Name him.

A Virgil Trucks, whose no-hit victories highlighted an otherwise drab 5-19 season in 1952.

The Detroit right-hander no-hit Washington 1-0 on May 15 and the Yankees 1-0 on Aug. 25 and nearly hurled another gem when he one-hit Washington in a 1-0 win on July 22. Discount those three games and Trucks would've finished the year with a 2-19 record and a 4.61 ERA.

The other pitchers to toss two no-hitters in a season? Chronologically, they are Cincinnati's Johnny Vander Meer (1938, in consecutive starts), Allie Reynolds of the Yankees (1951), Jim Maloney of the Reds (1965) and California's Nolan Ryan (1973).

Q This Pirate set the major league record for pinch-hit home runs—since broken—when he stepped off the bench and clubbed No. 15 on Aug. 21, 1963, off Chicago's Lindy McDaniel at Wrigley Field. Name him.

A Jerry Lynch, who finished with 18 pinch-hit homers during a 13-year career spent with the Bucs and Reds. Lynch currently ranks second on the all-time list behind Cliff Johnson (1972-86), who slugged 20.

Q Which Pirates manager later became an NFL head coach, the only individual to achieve this two-sport double?

A Hugo Bezdek, a native of Prague, then located in Austria-Hungary, today the capital of the Czech Republic. He debuted with the Bucs at the age of 34 in 1917 and guided the team to a 166-187 record in parts of three seasons.

Bezdek didn't fare nearly as well as the first coach of the Cleveland Rams, who joined the NFL in 1937: In his one and a half seasons at the helm, the Rams compiled a woeful 1-13 record.

Before managing the Pirates, Bezdek was better known for his exploits on the gridiron than on the diamond. He earned All-America honors (1905) as a fullback under the legendary Amos Alonzo Stagg at the University of Chicago and later coached at Arkansas, Oregon, Penn and Penn State. He led the Nittany Lions to a 65-30-11 record.

Penn State was unbeaten under Bezdek in 1920 and 1921 and his 1922 squad played in the Rose Bowl, the school's first postseason appearance. The Nittany Lions lost 14-3 to Southern Cal. A previous trip to Pasadena proved more enjoyable for Bezdek: He led Oregon to a 14-0 victory over Penn in the 1917 Rose Bowl.

Q Pittsburgh players have won 24 National League batting championships, but only once have Pirates finished 1-2 in the batting race. Which two Bucs were involved?

A Honus Wagner (.355) and Fred Clarke (.351), who were the league's top two hitters in 1903. Cincinnati's Mike Donlin officially tied Clarke for runner-up honors, although he was actually edged out for second, .3513-.3508, by the Pirates' player-manager.

Q The Pirates have been blessed with some outstanding defensive outfielders through the years. Which one holds the team record for assists in a season, with 32?

A Center fielder Max Carey, a scourge to opposing baserunners throughout his career, but especially in 1916. Carey piled up 339 assists in his 20 years of big league ball, a modern National League record.

EMERGENCY UMPIRES

The Pirates and Brooklyn played most of their Aug. 20, 1912, doubleheader at Forbes Field without an umpire in sight. A *real* umpire, that is.

One player from each team was pressed into service after injuries incapacitated the regular umps. Only two worked games back then.

When base umpire Bill Brennan tore knee ligaments while covering a first-inning play at second, plate ump Brick Owens was compelled to make all the calls. An inning later, a foul tip off the bat of Pittsburgh first baseman Dots Miller broke Owens' breastbone. Both umps were taken to St. John's Hospital.

Rather than call off the twinbill, each team agreed to supply an umpire. Brooklyn catcher Ed Phelps—a former Pirate—and Pittsburgh pinch-hit specialist Ham Hyatt worked the rest of the first game and all of the second, with nary a complaint from either side.

"They did excellent work," noted the *Pittsburgh Post*. "The only sign of displeasure was a dark look cast toward Phelps when he called a strike that greatly displeased [batter and teammate] Red Smith."

The Pirates won the first game 3-2 before losing the second, 9-1.

Q No one would consider him a strikeout pitcher in the mold of Nolan Ryan, Steve Carlton or Roger Clemens, yet he holds the Pirates' career record in that category. Name him.

A Bob Friend, who finished with 1,682 strikeouts. Friend's highest total in his 15 years with Pittsburgh was 183, in 1960. That was one of only two seasons in which he exceeded 150.

Q Now in his third tour of duty with the Pirates, he's known for needling opponents—musically. Name him.

A Vince Lascheid, the Three Rivers Stadium organist (1970-72, 1979-82, 1987-).

Lascheid once played *Silent Night* after Ray Knight of the Reds struck out with the bases loaded. He also improvised in 1979 after Chicago shortstop Ivan DeJesus committed a costly error, playing *What a Friend We Have in Jesus*. "I got letters on that one," Lascheid said with a mischievous glint in his eye.

He was also a thorn in the side of former All-Star first baseman Steve Garvey. Lascheid would play *There She is, Miss America* when Garvey approached the plate, alluding to the fact that Garvey always looked as if he had just stepped from a salon, not a hair out of place.

"Their P.R. guy told our P.R. guy to ask me not to play it, that Garvey didn't like it," Lascheid says. He gladly complied. The next time Garvey stepped up to the plate, Lascheid tapped out a different tune: Stevie Wonder's *Isn't She Lovely?*

Q This third baseman would've been a shoo-in for National League Rookie of the Year honors—had there been such an award in 1899. He batted .355, led the league with 27 triples (still the major league rookie record), finished third in RBIs (116), hits (219) and slugging percentage (.532), tied for third with nine home runs, scored 126 runs and stole 26 bases. Name this phenom.

A Jimmy Williams, who also put together a 27-game hitting streak, still the franchise record. Williams never matched any of his 1899 numbers again during an 11-year career.

Q Why did broadcaster Bob Prince abruptly dismiss 1960 World Series hero Bill Mazeroski after only one question in a nationally televised locker room interview following Game 7?

A He had no idea Maz had sunk the Yankees with a ninth-inning homer, the first Series-ending blast in history. What Prince later termed "my most monumental embarrassing moment as a broadcaster" stemmed from the back-and-forth nature of that deciding game.

Prince and his Yankees counterpart, Mel Allen, were part of the CBS-TV crew for the Series. CBS decreed that the winning team's broadcaster would conduct post-game interviews from the locker room.

When Pittsburgh grabbed a 9-7 lead in the eighth inning, Prince headed for the Pirates' clubhouse. Upon arriving, he was informed that the Yankees had tied the score and was told to rejoin his colleagues in the broadcasting booth.

But before he could fight his way back upstairs through the crush of people, a tremendous roar shook Forbes Field, indicating to Prince that the Pirates had prevailed. He promptly retraced his steps to the locker room, where a beaming Mazeroski was shoved in front of him.

"How does it feel to be a member of the world champions?" Prince asked.

"Great," Maz replied.

That was the extent of the interview.

"Two hectic hours later," Prince recalled, "I was having dinner with my wife, Betty. 'By the way,' I asked, 'just how did we finally win it?'"

"You must be kidding," she replied. "Maz hit a home run."

Said Prince, "I nearly fell off my chair."

Q Doe Boyland fanned in his first major league at bat on Sept. 4, 1978. What was unusual about that strikeout?

A Boyland was sitting on the bench at the time.

Manager Chuck Tanner called on the rookie first baseman, a left-handed batter, to face Mets right-hander Skip Lockwood. But when Lockwood injured his arm after the third pitch and exited the game, New York manager Joe Torre summoned lefty Kevin Kobel. Tanner, playing the percentages, replaced Boyland with right-handed batter Rennie Stennett, who inherited a 1-2 count.

Stennett whiffed, but under the rules of scoring, Boyland was saddled with the strikeout because he was in the batter's box for two of the three strikes.

Q When Barry Bonds slugged a three-run homer at Three Rivers Stadium on July 5, 1989, he and his father Bobby climbed to the top of the all-time father-son home run list with 408. The Bondses had been deadlocked with two father-son duos who also had Pittsburgh connections. Name them.

A Yogi and Dale Berra and Gus and Buddy Bell.

Infielder Dale Berra played with the Pirates (1977-84), as did outfielder Gus Bell (1950-52). What's more, Buddy Bell was born in Pittsburgh.

Barry Bonds hit his historic shot off San Francisco's Steve Bedrosian in the ninth inning of a 6-4 loss at Three Rivers Stadium. He shipped the bat to his father as a memento of their joint achievement.

Bobby (332) and Barry (411) had combined for 743 home runs entering the 1999 season.

Q In 1959, Pirates general manager Joe Brown spurned a trade offer by Kansas City involving two players who would later claim MVP honors. Name them.

A Pittsburgh shortstop Dick Groat and Athletics right fielder Roger Maris. In December of that year, KC sent Maris to the Yankees in a seven-player deal. Groat and Maris were their league's respective MVPs in 1960. Maris repeated in 1961, the year he slugged a then-record 61 home runs.

Q Which Pirates teammates later went into managing—managing women's teams, that is?

A Max Carey and Carson Bigbee, who guided clubs in the All-American Girls Professional Baseball League.

Chewing gum magnate Philip K. Wrigley—the long-time Cubs owner—founded the AAGPBL in 1943 to fill a void created when war-time military call-ups ravaged rosters on the big league level and forced many minor leagues to cease operations entirely. Ex-major leaguers were hired to direct several of the teams.

Carey managed the Milwaukee Chicks and the Fort Wayne Daisies, the focus of Penny Marshall's 1992 film on the AAGPBL, *A League of Their Own*. The Chicks ran away with the regular-season title in 1944 and then won the championship series in seven games. Bigbee managed the Springfield Sallies and the Muskegon Lassies.

Bigbee played in left field and Carey in center for most of their 11 seasons as Pirates teammates (1916-26).

THE MARATHON MAN

M anagers nowadays celebrate when a pitcher throws a complete game. But in 1955, Vernon Law threw the equivalent of *two* complete games in one night.

He wound up with nothing more than a tired arm and a no-decision.

Law worked 18 innings against Milwaukee at Forbes Field on July 19 because he dissuaded manager Fred Haney—on several occasions—from picking up the bullpen phone. Relief for Law didn't come until the 19th, when Haney figured he'd finally had enough. Bob Friend answered the call and immediately surrendered a run, but he emerged as the winner when the Pirates pushed across two runs in the bottom half of the inning.

Wrote Al Abrams of the *Pittsburgh Post-Gazette*, "He wasn't around when the 4-3 victory was pulled out of the smoldering embers of defeat in the 19th inning, but Vernon Law turned in a performance the equal of which the great pitching titans of the past would have been proud to call their own."

No big league pitcher since has worked as many as 18 innings in a game. In fact, no one's even come close.

What's incredible about Law's ironman feat is that he was working on three days' rest. Scheduled starter Ron Kline begged off because of a sore shoulder, so Haney pressed Law into service. He gave the Pirates nine strong innings . . . and plenty more.

"Fred kept asking me if I was OK. I kept saying I was fine," Law recalled. "He tried to pull me after 12 innings, then he tried again to pull me after 15. I said, 'Skip, after pitching this long, let me win it or lose it. You owe me that.' "

Five days later, Haney handed the ball to Law for a start against the Cubs. He again worked overtime—10 innings—but this time came away with a win.

Q Willie Stargell slugged more home runs (475) than any Pirates lefthander and Ralph Kiner holds the team record for righties (301). Name the franchise record-holder for switch-hit homers.

A Bobby Bonilla, who hit 114 from 1986 to 1991.

Q Until Bonilla came along, which player held the Pirates' single-season record for home runs by a switch-hitter?

A Left fielder Jim Russell, who hit 12 in 1945. Bonilla surpassed that mark in 1987 with 15 homers and boosted the standard to 32 in 1990.

Q Shortstops have won nine National League batting titles since the turn of the century. How many of those players were Pirates?

A All of them. Honus Wagner won an NL-record eight crowns from 1900 to 1911—seven of them as a shortstop—and Arky Vaughan (1935) and Dick Groat (1960) claimed the others.

Q This one-time Pirates farmhand never made it to the big leagues—at least not in baseball. He did become a power hitter in politics, serving three terms as governor of a prominent northeastern state. Name him.

A Mario Cuomo, who finished his final four-year term as governor of New York in 1995.

Young Mario Matthew Cuomo—he went by Matt back then—appeared in 81 games as an outfielder for the Pirates' Brunswick (Ga.) affiliate in the Georgia-Florida League in 1952, batting .244 with one homer and 26 RBIs.

Cuomo was batting a team-high .353 when he injured his wrist after slamming into the wall while in pursuit of a fly ball. Then, according to *Current Biography*, "a wild pitch that hospitalized him for a month convinced him that the major leagues were not in his future."

It's interesting to note that Cuomo signed for a $2,000 bonus—$900 more than the Yankees paid Mickey Mantle to affix his signature to a contract two years before.

Q During the 1977 season Chuck Tanner handed this manager—his future boss—his only major league defeat. Name him.

A Media mogul Ted Turner, the owner of the Atlanta Braves.

Following the Braves' 16th consecutive loss, Turner dispatched manager Dave Bristol on a scouting trip and appointed himself acting manager in an effort to discover why the team was playing so horribly. In his one day at the helm, Atlanta dropped a 2-1 decision to the Pirates at Three Rivers Stadium.

NL president Chub Feeney forced Turner to step down after one game, citing a league rule that prohibits a manager from owning part of his club. Bristol soon returned to finish out the year.

Tanner managed Turner's Braves from 1986 to 1988.

Q When the Apollo 11 crew returned home after exploring the lunar surface in 1969, a former Pirates pitcher offered this observation: "I'm anxious to see some of the moon-rock samples the astronauts brought back. I'm sure there are a few of my home run balls in that crowd." Who uttered those lines?

A Wilmer Mizell, a self-deprecating sort who spent parts of three seasons (1960-62) with Pittsburgh.

Q What was the exact time, day of the week and date of Bill Mazeroski's World Series-winning home run in 1960?

A 3:36 p.m., Thursday, Oct. 13.

Q What happened to home plate not long after Mazeroski stepped on it that momentous day?

A Squirrel Hill resident Michael J. "Red" Cipa, who had brought a shovel to the game in anticipation of a Pirates victory, dug up the plate and carted it home. Cipa was reportedly perturbed that he ruined an $85 sport coat in the process.

Q In what season did the Pirates set a franchise record with a 16-game winning streak?

A 1909. The pennant-bound Bucs also reeled off a 14-game streak that year, the third-longest in team history. Pittsburgh won 15 straight in 1903 en route to the National League title.

MAGIC ACT

F rancisco Cordova, Ricardo Rincon and Mark Smith were unlikely candidates to take part in something epic, given their undistinguished major league resumes.

But on the night of July 12, 1997, they took center stage in a magical performance that rocked Three Rivers Stadium to its foundation and focused the national spotlight on Pittsburgh. Cordova and Rincon threw the first combined extra-inning no-hitter in major league history as the Bucs beat Houston 3-0 on Smith's dramatic 10th-inning home run.

"What a night," gushed Pirates manager Gene Lamont. "You couldn't get a game more exciting."

A throng of 44,119 agreed, cheering louder with each passing inning. When Smith connected off Astros closer John Hudek, the roar was positively deafening.

Cordova held Houston hitless for nine masterful innings, but because the Bucs failed to score, his final line read: no runs, no hits, no decision. Rincon came on and threw a hitless 10th. Smith then followed walks to Jason Kendall and Turner Ward with a no-doubt blast off the facade of the third level seats in left field to not only win the game, but secure the seventh no-hitter in Pirates history as well.

"I knew as soon as I hit it," he said. "I can't describe the feeling. It's the greatest feeling you could ever have."

Cordova, born into poverty in the remote, mountainous Mexican village of Rancho Cerro Azul—he grew up in a hut with a thatched roof and mud floor—telephoned his father, Ernesto, with the news. The elder Cordova won 141 games during his Mexican League pitching career.

His son also hurled in the Mexican League. In fact, Cordova and Rincon were Mexico City Reds teammates in 1994 and 1995. Both arrived in the majors as nonroster players, Cordova in 1996, Rincon a year later. Along with Smith, who began the season in the minor leagues after the Bucs acquired him from San Diego in a little-noticed spring training deal, they made headlines in grand fashion.

Cordova, at the time a modest 10-12 for his career, was overpowering from the outset. The tension built to excruciating levels in the later innings.

"Oh, man, was I nervous," said Lou Collier, who was making only his seventh major league start at shortstop. "I've never felt like that in my life. You just feel so much pressure, every pitch. By the ninth, I was numb through my legs."

Cordova quickly retired the first two batters before nicking Chuck Carr with an inside fastball. He then induced the dangerous Jeff Bagwell to loft a lazy fly ball to right as the crowd erupted.

Unfortunately, because the Bucs didn't score in the bottom half of the inning, Lamont was forced to make an unpopular move. He pulled Cordova.

"You never want to take a guy out during a no-hitter, but it wasn't a hard decision for me," Lamont explained. "He'd thrown too many pitches [121]. You don't want him getting up there around the 140-pitch count."

Lamont summoned Rincon, who feared spoiling what his close friend had worked so hard to accomplish.

"I just hope everybody remembers the 10th inning and what Ricardo did," said pitching coach Pete Vuckovich. "I don't know if there's more pressure on Francisco or Ricardo. One minute, he's watching the game, like you or me, the next minute it's all on his shoulders."

But Rincon retired the Astros without incident, setting the stage for Smith. With one swing, the hulking pinch hitter propelled Cordova and Rincon into the record books and made a bit of history himself, too. Never before had a National League no-hitter ended with a home run.

Detroit's Virgil Trucks authored the only other major league no-hitter to end with a homer. Vic Wertz rocketed a Bob Porterfield pitch into the Tiger Stadium stands with two outs in the bottom of the ninth to give Trucks a 1-0 victory over Washington on May 15, 1952—and secure the first of his two no-hitters that season.

Q Pirates TV play-by-play announcer Greg Brown began his career with the club in what capacity?

A He was hired as the backup Pirate Parrot in 1979, the year the mascot was introduced. Brown later worked in the promotions department, served as the team's radio and television coordinator and worked as the stadium PA announcer. He joined the broadcast team in 1994 after five seasons as the Buffalo Bisons' play-by-play man.

Q Before Randy Johnson arrived in the majors, this Pirates pitcher held the distinction as the tallest player in big league history. Name him.

A Six-foot-nine Johnny Gee, who appeared in 25 games for the Bucs between his rookie year of 1939 and 1944, when he was sold to the New York Giants. Gee compiled a 5-8 record and a 4.64 ERA while with Pittsburgh.

The 6-10 Johnson, who won the 1995 Cy Young award as the ace of Seattle's staff, debuted with the Expos in 1988. He was compelled to share his honor as the tallest player in major league history when pitcher Eric Hillman joined the Mets in 1992.

Q This pitcher found little success in parts of four seasons (1962-65) with the Pirates, compiling a 2-3 record, but he contributed to a multitude of victories as the athletic director at Duke University. Name him.

A Tom Butters, who stepped down as the Blue Devils' AD in 1998 after 21 years in charge.

Butters joined the Duke staff in 1967 as director of special events and later coached the baseball team for three seasons (1968-70). One of his best decisions as AD was to hire Mike Krzyzewski as head basketball coach.

Since 1986, Krzyzewski has steered the Blue Devils to two national championships and six title game appearances, twice as many as any other school in that time. Duke has also reached the Final Four on eight occasions over the last 14 seasons, more than anyone else.

Q Which object employed to hex the opposition did broadcaster Bob Prince popularize in 1966?

A The Green Weenie.

The Pirates were playing in Houston and the Astros' dangerous Lee May was batting with the bases loaded when Prince noticed that Pittsburgh trainer Danny Whelan had taped a hot dog, which he'd taken from the pre-game clubhouse spread, to the dugout railing in an effort to hex the Astros. May popped out and Green Weenie mania was born.

Prince wielded a green rubber hot dog from the broadcast booth the rest of the season, invoking its "powers" in critical situations. The Green Weenie nearly carried the Pirates to a championship that year—they finished in third place, only three games behind the pennant-winning Dodgers.

Q Shortstop Dal Maxvill uttered the following line when an imposing physical specimen joined the Pirates in July of 1973: "I don't know who he is, but I'm glad he's on our side." To whom was Maxvill referring?

A Outfielder Dave Parker, quite a sight at 6-5, 230 pounds.

Q What was the significance of right fielder Mike Mitchell's home run for Cincinnati at Pittsburgh on July 5, 1909?

A It was the first homer hit at Forbes Field, then less than a week old. Mitchell connected during the second game of a morning-afternoon doubleheader, supplying the only run in a 6-1 loss.

Q Who hit the Pirates' first home run at the new ballpark?

A Rookie second baseman Dots Miller, who went deep on July 29, some three weeks after Mitchell's blast.

The Pirates spent most of the intervening time on the road, playing at New York, Brooklyn, Boston and Philadelphia. The prolonged trip was so grueling that owner Barney Dreyfuss treated his players to an afternoon at the shore. The team traveled by train to Atlantic City, N.J., on an open date during its stay in Philadelphia.

Several days later, Miller's homer highlighted a 4-3 victory over the Phillies. It was the first home run to actually leave the park.

"In the fourth inning Miller knocked the ball over the left field fence," noted the *Pittsburg Gazette Times*. "It was the first ball that cleared the fence at Forbes Field. Mitchell of the Cincinnati Reds made a home run some time ago, but the ball hit the coping of the green wall and bounded out of sight."

Q Who hit the Pirates' first home run at Exposition Park?

A Right fielder Fred Carroll, who victimized Chicago during an 11-8 victory on April 24, 1891—the year *after* the park was opened. Jocko Fields, an outfielder who spent parts of four seasons with the Pirates (1887-89, 1891), was the first player to homer at Exposition Park.

Fields' homer came on June 10, 1890, when he was a member of Pittsburgh's Players League club. The Bucs did not become a tenant of the ballpark until the following season.

Moments after Carroll struck the first Pirates home run at Exposition Park, left fielder Pete Browning hit the second. Both were inside-the-park blows. A *Pittsburg Post* account offered the following description:

"The two four-baggers were made in the eighth inning, one after the other, and were clean-cut and full-sized, though both Carroll and Browning were compelled to turn on full steam to beat the ball to the plate."

THE CARDBOARD MASTERPIECE

H onus Wagner never even came close to earning $451,000 during his 21-year major league career. But his baseball card did.

The 1^{1}/$_2$-by-2^{1}/$_2$-inch multi-colored cardboard card, in mint condition, fetched $451,000 during an auction at Sotheby's in New York City on March 22, 1991. Los Angeles Kings owner Bruce McNall and his star player, Wayne Gretzky, outbid Colorado dealer Mark Friedland, who predicted the card would eventually double in value.

"I think it can go for a million, personally," said Friedland. "To me, this is a historical document or a historical piece of memorabilia as much as it is a baseball card."

Reportedly, only two are in mint condition.

"It's the ultimate collectable," said Peter J. Siegal, a collector from Manhattan. "There's nothing more valuable."

That's due to the scarcity of the item. Piedmont Cigarettes issued a set of cards in 1910 with color likenesses of the day's great players. The reverse side bore an advertisement for Piedmont, "the cigarette of quality."

Wagner asked the company to withdraw his cards, but no one knows precisely why. The request was not made because he didn't smoke; he did. Presumably, Wagner was concerned about perceptions that he was encouraging the use of tobacco, especially among children.

Piedmont acceded to Wagner's wishes and withdrew as many cards as possible. Few were circulated; fewer still survive. An estimated 40 are in existence.

Incidentally, Friedland's prediction might well materialize one day soon. The card McNall and Gretzky purchased in 1991 was sold five years later by Christie's Fine Art Auctioneers in New York to an anonymous buyer—for $580,000.

Q This Pirates right fielder and manager was instrumental in bringing Babe Ruth to the major leagues. Name him.

A Patsy Donovan, who hit .307 and scored 100 or more runs six times for the Bucs between 1892 and 1899 and managed the team in 1897 and 1899.

As a Red Sox scout, Donovan urged Boston owner Joe Lannin to sign a promising pitcher from Baltimore named George Herman Ruth. Lannin took his advice.

Ruth reached the majors in 1914 and pitched the Red Sox to three world championships (1915, 1916 and 1918) before Lannin's successor, New York theatrical entrepreneur Harry Frazee, sold him to the Yankees in a bid to finance his musical, *No! No! Nanette*. Ruth celebrated four more world titles in New York, as an outfielder.

Q This Cincinnati outfielder hit three consecutive home runs against the Pirates in a dramatic 13-inning slugfest at Crosley Field on Aug. 12, 1966, yet it wasn't enough to prevent a 14-11 Pittsburgh victory. Name him.

A Art Shamsky. Ironically, Shamsky entered the game for defensive purposes. He slugged a two-run homer in the bottom of the eighth, a solo shot in the 10th to tie the score and a two-run blast in the 11th to retie it.

"I was lucky to hit any of those home runs," said Shamsky. "I was just trying to meet the ball. It was just one of those days when everything I did was right."

Nothing went right for the pitchers. The teams equaled a major league record by combining for 11 homers (the Bucs socked six). There were 29 hits in all, along with 18 walks, off of 11 pitchers in the four-hour, 22-minute marathon.

"It was the wildest game I've ever looked at," said Pittsburgh manager Harry Walker. In a delicious bit of irony, his Pirates won the slugfest when Manny Mota rapped a 150-foot single that knocked in two runs and snapped an 11-11 tie.

Shamsky tied an individual big league mark two days later when he slugged a pinch-hit homer against Vernon Law, again in a losing cause. That gave him home runs in four consecutive at bats.

Q Which Pirates broadcaster once succeeded a future United States president?

A Jim Woods, who served as Bob Prince's right-hand man from 1958 through 1969.

Woods was working at KGLO in Mason City, Iowa, in the late 1930s when Ronald Reagan—then known as "Dutch"—left his job as the voice of University of Iowa football after signing a Hollywood contract. Woods was hired as his replacement.

Reagan appeared in some 50 films before turning to politics. He served as governor of California before winning election in 1980 as the 40th president of the United States.

Q This Pirates pitcher got off to a wild start against Cincinnati on May 1, 1974, hitting the game's first three batters. Who was responsible for this dubious achievement?

A Dock Ellis. He plunked Pete Rose, Joe Morgan and Dan Driessen before an exasperated Danny Murtaugh removed him. Ellis threw only 12 pitches, none of them strikes.

"I've never seen anyone that wild," said Reds manager Sparky Anderson, whose team won the game, 5-3.

Ironically, Ellis had hit only one batter previously that season and only one the year before. He equaled a major league record by beaning three batters in a single inning.

Q What National League record did Jason Kendall set during the 1998 season?

A Most stolen bases by a catcher (26), eclipsing the old mark of 25 set by John Stearns of the Mets in 1978. Kansas City's John Wathan established the major league standard of 32 in 1982.

Only two catchers in big league history have exceeded Kendall's total: Wathan, who also swiped 28 bases in 1983, and Ray Schalk of the White Sox, who pilfered 30 in 1916.

Kendall swiped his 26th at San Francisco's 3Com Park on Sept. 22 and then scored the Bucs' only run in an 8-1 loss. The grounds crew presented him with the second base bag as a keepsake.

"Every base he stole meant something," said manager Gene Lamont. "I don't think he cared about the record at all."

Kendall was on a pace to shatter Wathan's standard in 1999—he'd swiped 22 bases in 80 games—when he dislocated his right ankle and tore ligaments in a gruesome mishap at first base July 4 against Milwaukee. Even that total, achieved in half a season, ranks 10th on the catchers' all-time single-season list.

Incidentally, until Kendall arrived in Pittsburgh, the club record for stolen bases by a catcher was 12, by Tony Pena in 1984 and 1985.

Q Which musician turned *Beat 'em, Bucs* into a regional hit in 1960?

A Benny Benack, a local trumpet player. He and his Dixieland combo, the Iron City Six, recorded the fight song that summer and it became a smash hit (Benack appropriated the tune to *Camptown Races*, written by Pittsburgh native Stephen Foster). The Iron City Six rode around town in a flatbed truck, drumming up support for the Pirates, and often serenaded fans before games at Forbes Field.

Q What does former Pirates shortstop Dick Groat have in common with such greats as Ernie Banks, Bob Feller, Al Kaline, Sandy Koufax, Mel Ott and Dave Winfield that sets him apart from most other players in major league history?

A He never spent a day in the minor leagues. Groat, a so-called bonus baby, debuted with the Pirates at the age of 21 on June 19, 1952, after leading Duke University into the College World Series. He hit a team-high .284 in 95 games with the Bucs.

Q No player in Pirates history has gained membership in the exclusive 20-20-20 club: 20 or more doubles, triples and home runs in a given season. Who came closest?

A Kiki Cuyler, who finished with 43 doubles, 26 triples and 18 home runs in 1925, his second full season in the big leagues. He never hit as many triples or home runs again.

Only four major leaguers have produced 20-20-20 seasons since Cuyler's near miss in 1925: Cardinals first baseman and National League MVP Jim Bottomley in 1928 (42 doubles, 20 triples, 31 homers); Cleveland outfielder Jeff Heath in 1941 (32-20-24); New York Giants outfielder Willie Mays in 1957 (26-20-35); and Kansas City third baseman George Brett in 1979 (42-20-23).

Q Name the Pirates outfielder who smashed the first World Series home run.

A Jimmy Sebring, who connected against Boston's Cy Young in Game 1 on Oct. 1, 1903, helping the Pirates to a 7-3 victory. Sebring was clearly a long shot to achieve long-ball fame: He hit only six homers in his five-year major league career.

FROM SHAME TO FAME

P itcher Burleigh Grimes began his Hall of Fame career with the Pirates, but he hardly looked the part of a baseball immortal in 1917, his first full season in the majors.

Grimes struggled to a 3-16 record and lost 13 consecutive games that year, still a franchise record. Consequently, no tears were shed in Pittsburgh when he was shipped to Brooklyn in a five-player offseason deal.

But Grimes reversed his fortunes with the Dodgers and was an established winner by the time he returned to Pittsburgh in 1928. He tied for the major league lead in victories (25) and complete games (28) that season, led the National League in innings ($330^2/_3$), tied for the NL lead in shutouts (4) and even batted a career-high .321.

Grimes finished his career in 1934 with 270 wins. That total likely seemed incomprehensible back in the dark days of 1917, when he seemed destined for a return to the minors—not a place in Cooperstown.

Q Which Pirates farmhand once slugged 66 home runs in a season?

A Dick Stuart, who led the Class A Western League in home runs and RBIs (158) in 1956 while playing for Lincoln (Neb.). Recalling his exploits years later, Stuart said, "If the pitching was better I'd have hit 90 home runs. I had to chase a lot of bad pitches to get those homers."

His homeric feats garnered attention of a sort rarely seen in the low minors. And Stuart—a brash sort described by *Life* magazine as an "irrepressible egotist"—ate it up.

"I had 60 [home runs] after 100 games," he recalled. "Everyone in America was calling me. Then I stopped hitting them and I stopped getting calls."

Though Stuart went into a mild tailspin at the close of the season, he still managed to set league records for home runs, RBIs and total bases (385) and finish with a .297 average.

Stuart's total of 66 homers, incidentally, ranks him fourth on the all-time single-season minor league list behind Joe Bauman, who slugged 72 for Roswell (N.M.) of the Longhorn League in 1954; Bob Crues, who hit 69 for Amarillo, Texas, of the West Texas-New Mexico League in 1948; and Joe Hauser, who cracked 69 for Minneapolis (Minn.) of the American Association in 1933. Only Stuart and Hauser reached the majors.

Q Which Pirate knocked in the deciding run in Game 7 of the 1971 World Series, scoring Willie Stargell from first base with an eighth-inning hit-and-run double?

A Third baseman Jose Pagan, whose two-bagger gave the Bucs a 2-0 advantage en route to a 2-1 victory. Roberto Clemente's fourth-inning solo home run off Mike Cuellar put Pittsburgh ahead to stay.

Q This former Pirate ranks as the most prolific pinch hitter ever. He finished his career in 1982 with 150 pinch hits—a major league record—and a .297 average as a batter off the bench. Name him.

A Manny Mota, an outfielder with the Bucs from 1963 to 1968. He spent 13 of his 20 seasons with the Dodgers.

Mota refined his pinch-hitting prowess when he realized the odds against breaking into the lineup. With Roberto Clemente, Willie Stargell, Bill Virdon and, later, Matty Alou in the outfield, opportunities to start were limited.

Rather than pout, Mota worked diligently to become an adept pinch hitter. Eleven times in his career he delivered at better than a .300 clip off the bench, including a high (minimum of 20 at bats) of .400 in 1972.

130

Q Which Pirates center fielder went 6-for-6 against Philadelphia in an 1899 game, yet never hit the ball out of the infield?

A Ginger Beaumont, who beat out six infield hits July 22 at Exposition Park as the Pirates pounded the Phils, 18-4. He also scored six times to equal a National League record.

"Beaumont's hitting was the feature of the game," reported the *Pittsburg Post*. "Six times he faced [pitcher Wiley] Piatt, and six times he dumped the ball and beat it to first. Not one of Beaumont's hits yesterday went out of the diamond. He dumped them in all directions, and then fairly shot to first. Three times his speed was such that the ball was not thrown."

Beaumont was the second Pirate to bang out six hits in a game. The first was center fielder Jacob Stenzel, who went 6-for-6 in a 20-4 victory over Boston at Exposition Park on May 14, 1896.

Q The Pirates once traded their starting catcher for a former outfielder who had retired as a player—14 years before. Name the two individuals involved in this unusual swap.

A Manny Sanguillen and Chuck Tanner. The Bucs traded Sanguillen and $100,000 to the Oakland Athletics on Nov. 5, 1976, in exchange for Tanner, who had managed the A's to a second-place finish that season.

"[Oakland owner] Charlie Finley called me and said, 'The Pirates asked for permission to talk to you. They offered us Manny Sanguillen or $100,000,' " Tanner recalled. "So he said, 'They really want you—I'm gonna ask 'em for both.' I said, 'You can't, that's not fair.' He said, 'They'll give it to me.' And they did."

Funny thing, the Bucs reacquired Sanguillen—in a conventional players-for-players trade—on April 4, 1978. Tanner managed the Pirates through the 1985 season.

Q Which Pirate did management persuade to "take the pledge"—with disastrous results?

A Paul Waner, who was known to enjoy a drink or two—or more.

Prior to the 1938 season, team officials talked Waner into going on the wagon, convinced that his performance would improve accordingly. They misjudged the situation terribly.

A year after batting .354, a dry Waner dipped under .300 for the first time in his career, finishing at .280. Waner resumed his drinking—and his hitting (.328)—the following season.

Forbes Field old-timers recalled Waner showing up at the ballpark before games glassy-eyed after a night of imbibing, announcing "3-for-4 today," and then doing just that.

Q This Pirate broke out of a six-week long-ball slump in a big way, slugging a record three home runs in Game 2 of the 1971 National League Championship Series. Name him.

A First baseman Bob Robertson, whose explosion at the expense of the Giants on Oct. 3 ended a home run drought stretching back to Aug. 25.

"This is the best day I've ever had," said Robertson. "I've never hit three home runs in a game before, except maybe in Pony League."

Robertson followed with another homer his first time up in Game 3. He set League Championship Series records for most home runs in a game and most home runs in series (4) and equaled LCS standards for most runs in a game (4), most runs in a series (5) and most RBIs in a game (5).

Q What was Monument Hill?

A A bluff on the North Side overlooking Exposition Park, which provided an excellent vantage point for those fans who didn't wish to pay their way into a game. Because of the grandstands, these nonpaying patrons could only see a portion of the field, but that didn't stop them from congregating in large numbers.

"On warm days the hill was packed with spectators perched on the rocky ledges," wrote William M. Rimmel, whose story, "The early days of Pirate baseball," appeared in the *Pittsburgh Post-Gazette* on the eve of Three Rivers Stadium's 1970 debut. "And on Saturdays or holidays, a fellow had to be there hours before game time to be assured of finding a seat."

Q This player smacked 35 home runs for Hollywood and won Pacific Coast League MVP honors in 1953, but the talent-starved Pirates didn't even see fit to promote him in 1954. Name him.

A First baseman Dale Long. General manager Branch Rickey decided Long, then 28, needed additional seasoning following a year in which he also knocked in 116 runs, scored 106 and batted .272. Long was doomed to spend another season in the PCL.

"I was there so long," he said, "I asked Mr. Rickey if he wanted me to become president of the league."

Long finally earned a starting position with the Pirates in 1955.

No-Shows

O ne of the Pirates' easiest victories ever was recorded on May 10, 1892, when the New York Giants refused to play a scheduled game at Exposition Park. The Bucs never even broke a sweat in registering the first forfeit win in Pittsburgh history.

Nearly 500 spectators appeared on an overcast, threatening day, expecting to witness a game despite the rain showers that had fallen earlier. Turns out they stayed longer than the Giants.

"At 4 o'clock, the time advertised for the game to begin, rain came down, umbrellas went up and the players of both teams ran off the field for shelter," noted the *Pittsburg Post*. "In five minutes the rain stopped, and a few moments later, the gong sounded to begin play. The Pittsburg players responded, but not a Giant came in sight."

The team, in fact, was preparing to leave the premises. Umpire Jimmy Macullar approached the Giants' omnibus just as it was pulling out and pleaded with manager Pat Powers and his players to return, but they declined, claiming the diamond was unfit for play. Macullar thereupon declared Pittsburgh the victor.

"The grounds were quite muddy, but the base-lines and other positions were well covered with sawdust," noted the *Pittsburg Commercial Gazette*. "Umpire Macullar said the grounds were fit to play upon and there was ample time without rain in which to have finished a game [in fact, raindrops held off until 10 p.m.]. He said that if a club would jump up and leave the grounds under such circumstances, the public would have no protection whatsoever, and no assurance that a game was going to be played after quitting their business and going to the grounds."

Even Giants fans took a dim view of their team's premature departure.

"The refusal of the New Yorks to play at Pittsburg because of wet grounds, thereby forfeiting the game to Pittsburg, was unfavorably commented upon yesterday by local enthusiasts," noted the *New York Herald*. "The majority of the cranks [interviewed] were of the opinion that the New Yorks had acted as though they were afraid of defeat."

Crank was a 19th-century term for fan.

Q Which Pirate earned All-Star MVP honors by going 1-for-3 with an RBI at the plate and gunning down two American League baserunners from right field?

A No, not Roberto Clemente. Dave Parker, the Bucs' lone representative in their world championship year of 1979, was the hero of the National League's 7-6 victory at Seattle.

Parker threw out Boston's Jim Rice trying for a leadoff triple in the seventh and snuffed out another AL threat an inning later by nailing California's Brian Downing, who was attempting to score from second on a single. Said NL coach Chuck Tanner—Parker's manager—of his pegs, "They were right out of a howitzer."

Q This Pirate pitched at Forbes Field, just as his father had done a generation before—in the uniform of a Negro Leagues dynasty, the Homestead Grays. Name him.

A Bob Veale (1962-72), who followed in the footsteps of his father, Robert Sr. The elder Veale pitched many a game at Forbes Field, since the Grays were a regular tenant between 1939 and 1948.

Q What was the Crow's Nest?

A The third tier of stands at Forbes Field, which was hastily constructed in anticipation of the 1938 World Series. Unfortunately, the Cubs overtook the Pirates in the final week of the season, crushing Pittsburgh's Series hopes.

Q This first baseman started on the Pirates' dreadful 1952 team, although he's better known for the 19 years he spent on the bench— as the Bucs' trainer. Name him.

A Tony Bartirome, who batted .220 with no home runs and 16 RBIs as a 20-year-old rookie in 1952. That was Bartirome's only season in the majors, although his service to the club actually spanned 20 years. He was Pittsburgh's trainer from 1967 to 1985 before leaving for Atlanta with manager Chuck Tanner, under whom he coached for three seasons.

Q Name the only player to smash a home run over the 457-foot mark at Forbes Field, the deepest part of the park.

A Dick Stuart, whose tape-measure shot off Glen Hobbie of the Cubs on June 5, 1959, traveled an estimated 500 feet.

"The reaction of the fellows on the bench was sort of a numb feeling," said teammate Dick Groat following the 10-5 loss. "We couldn't conceive of anybody hitting a ball that far here. We shook our heads in bewilderment."

Stuart's mind-boggling strength came naturally, it seems. He spurned weight training, once cracking that his most strenuous lifting was done with an Iron City bottle in hand. Besides beer, Stuart drank an odd concoction at the suggestion of his father-in-law, who insisted it increased strength. Twice a day he dutifully gulped down a mixture of hot water, two teaspoons of honey and two teaspoons of vinegar.

Q Name the winning pitcher in the last World Series game played by the Pirates.

A Grant Jackson, who hurled two and two-thirds innings of scoreless, hitless relief in a 4-1 Game 7 victory over Baltimore in 1979. Jackson had pitched *for* the Orioles *against* Pittsburgh in the 1971 World Series.

Q Which Pirates Hall of Famer is acknowledged as the first major leaguer to regularly employ the basket catch on fly balls?

A Roberto Clemente? No, Rabbit Maranville, a shortstop with the Pirates (1921-24) and four other clubs. Maranville popularized the basket catch before its chief practitioners, Clemente and Willie Mays, were even born.

Q What do former Pirates Paul Waner and Jeff King have in common with only nine other players in major league history?

A They hit into unassisted triple plays.

Chicago shortstop Jimmy Cooney victimized the Bucs on June 30, 1927, at Forbes Field when he snared Waner's liner, stepped on second base to retire Lloyd Waner and then tagged the approaching Clyde Barnhart.

Philadelphia second baseman Mickey Morandini, a native of nearby Leechburg, entered the record book on Sept. 20, 1992, at Three Rivers Stadium when he speared King's line drive, stepped on second to double up Andy Van Slyke and then tagged Barry Bonds coming down from first base.

Morandini's unassisted triple play was the first in the National League since Cooney's.

Q This veteran became the first pitcher since Cy Young to throw no-hitters in both leagues, so his acquisition by the Pirates on Dec. 15, 1967, was heralded as a move that could bring a pennant to Pittsburgh. But back injuries hampered him in a 4-14 season and the club finished a disappointing sixth. Name this Hall of Famer.

A Jim Bunning, who no-hit Boston in 1958 while with the Tigers and threw a perfect game against the Mets in 1964 as a member of the Phillies—the first perfect game in the majors since Harvey Haddix's 1959 gem and the first perfect game victory in the National League since 1880.

Bunning never did regain his dominating form after the Phils traded him to Pittsburgh in exchange for infielder Don Money, pitcher Woody Fryman and minor league hurlers Hal Clem and Bill Laxton. He stumbled to a 14-23 record in a Pirates uniform and was dealt to the Dodgers for two minor leaguers and cash on Aug. 15, 1969.

ROAD KILL

T he 1890 Pirates rank among the worst road teams in major league history. They were, well, rank.

The Bucs, a bad club at home, turned positively wretched away from Recreation Park. In fact, they established a record for futility that will likely never be eclipsed—41 consecutive road losses.

Pittsburgh beat the Brooklyn Bridegrooms 7-5 at Washington Park on July 17 before launching its record streak against Brooklyn the following day with a 17-7 setback. The drought reached 41 games following a doubleheader defeat at Cincinnati on Sept. 12 that boosted the Bucs' season total to 100 losses. The Pirates bounced back the next day and dispatched the Reds 8-6 at League Park.

Road victories—victories of any kind—were few and far between for the 1890 Pirates, who drew so poorly at home that team officials opted to play almost the final third of the schedule away from home. The Bucs wound up playing 97 road games, losing 88 en route to a 23-113 record.

Incredible as it seems, those disgraceful figures were eclipsed later in the decade by an even more abominable team, the Cleveland Spiders. The Spiders finished 20-134 in 1899, due in large measure to 101 losses in their 112 road games.

Q Which Pirates relief pitcher was bitten by Cincinnati's Pedro Borbon during a 1974 brawl at Three Rivers Stadium?

A Daryl Patterson, who was given a tetanus shot afterwards as a precaution.

The benches emptied in the second game of a July 14 doubleheader when Jack Billingham hit Bucs starter Bruce Kison with a pitch. Borbon and Patterson squared off, with Patterson receiving the worst of the scrap: a black eye and an angry red mark on his left side.

"Borbon pulled my hair and bit me," Patterson said. "He hit me from the blind side after I let him go. He fights like a woman."

It took the umpires 20 minutes to restore order. Pittsburgh won the second game 2-1 after losing the opener 3-2. A split decision, in other words.

Q This shortstop filled in spectacularly when Dick Groat broke his wrist during the Pirates' stretch run to the pennant in 1960, batting .381 from the time of Groat's injury until the eventual MVP returned to the lineup. Who was the Bucs' MVB—Most Valuable Backup—that year?

A Dick Schofield, who took over at shortstop after a Lew Burdette pitch put Groat out of commission on Sept. 6. Schofield, who had played only sparingly until then, rose to the challenge and went 24-for-63 at the plate in a starting role.

"We thought it was a tremendous blow when Groat got hurt, but Schofield did a super job," said pitcher Bob Friend. "If he didn't perform like he did, we probably wouldn't have won the pennant."

Groat returned in time to appear in the final three games of the regular season, the last two as a starter.

Schofield finally shed his understudy role in 1963—his 11th major league season—after Groat was traded to the Cardinals.

Q What 1951 movie, which chronicled the transformation of the lowly Pirates into champions—with some heavenly assistance—used Forbes Field as a backdrop?

A *Angels in the Outfield*, starring Paul Douglas as a hard-hearted, hard-headed manager who leads his inept players to a pennant, with the help of unseen angels. Janet Leigh, Donna Corcoran and Keenan Wynn co-starred.

Q Which Pirate did Leigh date briefly while *Angels in the Outfield* was filmed in Pittsburgh?

A Ralph Kiner.

Q Name the only two players to homer in their first major league at bat as Pirates.

A Outfielder Walter Mueller and catcher Don Leppert, who later served on the team's coaching staff (1968-76).

Mueller took Chicago's Grover Cleveland Alexander deep on May 7, 1922, becoming the seventh big leaguer to slug a first-at bat home run. He was to hit only one other homer in his four-year career, spent exclusively with the Bucs.

Leppert touched up Curt Simmons of the Cardinals in the first game of a June 18, 1961, doubleheader at Forbes Field. He took the first five pitches, running the count to 3-2, before connecting with his first big league swing.

"I hit one my last time at bat in organized ball, too," Leppert said, "but I didn't hit too many in between."

Q Second baseman Bill Mazeroski formed half of the National League's premier double play combination in the mid-1960s. Name his partner.

A Shortstop Gene Alley, who won Gold Gloves in 1966 and 1967.

Alley and Mazeroski helped the Pirates lead the major leagues in double plays four times during their five seasons as a team, narrowly missing a fifth title when Philadelphia edged Pittsburgh by one in 1968. The Bucs' total of 215 double plays in 1966 still stands as a National League record.

Pittsburgh turned two so often because Mazeroski was a veritable magician in making the pivot at second base. The ball barely settled in his mitt before it was hurtling toward first base.

A few years ago several Pirates watching film of Mazeroski turning double plays marveled at his fluid, lightning-quick release. Only later did they learn the film had been slowed. At regular speed his catch and release was a blur.

Maz holds major league records for double plays by a second baseman in a career (1,706) and a season (161 in 1966) and most seasons leading the league in double plays (8).

Q This player ranks second on the Pirates' modern-day career batting list with a .336 average (Paul Waner leads at .340), yet he never won a batting title. Name him.

A Kiki Cuyler, who hit .354 and .357 with the Bucs in 1924 and 1925 and .360 and .355 with the Cubs in 1929 and 1930, but was shut out when it came to batting crowns. In fact, he never finished higher than third in the league.

Q Who hit the last home run at Forbes Field?

A Pirates right fielder Al Oliver, who slugged a solo homer in the second game of a June 28, 1970, doubleheader against Chicago, won 4-1 by the Bucs. Oliver's first-inning shot into the lower deck in right field came off Milt Pappas.

ON THE BRINK OF PERFECTION

Few pitchers in major league history have retired 27 consecutive batters in a game. Fewer still are hurlers who have done so and not finished with a no-hitter.

Woody Fryman and Jim Bibby of the Pirates each came within one pitch of perfection, but scratch hits by the first batters they faced spoiled their bid for no-hitters even before they got started. Fryman tamed the Mets 12-0 on July 1, 1966; Bibby beat the Braves 5-0 on May 19, 1981.

Ron Hunt led off against Fryman with an infield single and, moments later, was cut down by catcher Jim Pagliaroni trying to steal. Shortstop Gene Alley charged Hunt's slow bouncer over the mound, but he bobbled the ball and couldn't make a throw.

"I thought if the ball had been hit harder Gene could have thrown him out," said Fryman. "But it was hit slow and Hunt can run pretty good. I thought it was a hit."

His near-gem highlighted a sensational rookie season. The 26-year-old left-hander was in only his second season of pro ball. In fact, Fryman had been farming tobacco in his native Kentucky exactly one year earlier, before the Bucs signed him and he reported to their Batavia (N.Y.) farm club.

Fryman's best performance prior to the one-hitter was a three-hit 2-0 victory over Philadelphia in his previous start. He faced only 29 batters.

Noted Leonard Koppett of *The New York Times*, "It's quite possible, and even probable, that no other pitcher in major league history has ever displayed such efficiency for two starts in succession—54 outs in 56 batters."

Bibby's bid for perfection was spoiled when Atlanta's Terry Harper led off the game with what Pirates manager Chuck Tanner termed "a parachute over the infield." The ball fell safely between second baseman Phil Garner and right fielder Mike Easler.

"It's funny," said Harper. "When I hit it, I thought it was a good sign. I thought this was going to be a day of hitting for our team."

He couldn't have been more mistaken. Bibby retired the final 27 batters in order, wrapping up the one-hitter by inducing Harper to loft a fly to Easler.

"His control was incredible," said catcher Steve Nicosia. "I just sat outside and he hit the mitt 95 percent of the time."

In some ways, Bibby suggested, he was more dominating than in his no-hitter against Oakland in 1973, when he was a member of the Texas Rangers.

"I was a little more in command tonight than the time I threw the no-hitter," Bibby said. "I struck out 13 batters, I think, in the no-hitter, but I walked a few, too."

Incidentally, Bibby outhit the Braves all by himself. He contributed a pair of doubles to the Pittsburgh attack.

Q Despite a losing record and a hefty ERA during the regular season, manager Chuck Tanner tabbed this pitcher to start Game 5 of the 1979 World Series—a crucial contest given Baltimore's three games-to-one advantage. The result: five strong innings en route to a 7-1 victory that turned the Series in Pittsburgh's favor. Name this hurler.

A Jim Rooker, who later became a Pirates broadcaster.

Rooker was 4-7 with a 4.59 ERA during the season, but he answered the call in Game 5, permitting Baltimore only one run and three hits. Rooker didn't win the contest—the Bucs scored all seven runs in support of reliever Bert Blyleven—but he at least kept the Bucs close.

"The big difference in the Series? Rooker," said Orioles catcher Rick Dempsey after Pittsburgh swept the last three games to win the championship.

Q What term did writers and fans sometimes apply to the Pirates of the early 1950s?

A The Rickey Dinks, a play on the term rinky-dink and the name of the Bucs' general manager, Branch Rickey, who only occasionally—and grudgingly—loosened his club's purse strings.

For example, Rickey was seemingly reluctant to replace injured players with others who would require salaries and travel expenses. The team twice went on road trips during the 1952 season with only 18 players, seven under the limit. What's more, many Pirates during the Rickey regime toiled for the minimum major league salary.

Not even slugger Ralph Kiner, the club's chief drawing card, was immune from his boss' parsimonious ways. When Kiner demanded a raise, a disgusted Rickey responded with a trade threat—one he ultimately carried out. "We finished last with you," Rickey told Kiner. "We can finish last without you."

Q What does rookie Warren Morris have in common with former All-Star Bill Mazeroski—besides the fact that both have started at second base for the Pirates?

A They slugged bottom-of-the-ninth home runs to win championships. Maz's momentous blow snapped a 9-9 tie and beat the Yankees 10-9 in Game 7 of the 1960 World Series. Morris erased an 8-7 deficit and lifted Louisiana State to a 9-8 victory over Miami (Fla.) in the title game of the 1996 College World Series at Rosenblatt Stadium in Omaha, Neb.

The two homer heroes compared notes prior to the 1999 season when Mazeroski spent two weeks at the Bucs' Bradenton spring training camp as an infield instructor.

"I asked him about his homer and he said, 'Oh, it was nothing like yours,' " Mazeroski said. "I told him, 'The heck it wasn't, it was just as big.' "

Morris remains unconvinced, however.

"We're not even in the same ballpark," he said. "My homer doesn't even come close to his. What he did was one of the greatest moments in baseball history."

While Morris downplays his blast—the only homer he hit for LSU that year, ironically enough—it did provide arguably the most dramatic finish in the history of the College World Series, which dates to 1947. Several Miami players collapsed on the diamond in stunned disbelief as Morris circled the bases with the run that sealed LSU's third national championship in six years. The resulting mob scene at home plate was reminiscent of a similar one in Pittsburgh 36 years before, when another second baseman was engulfed by a wave of delirious teammates.

"It's unbelievable," Morris said afterwards. "I really don't remember what happened from the time I touched first base until I touched home. The only reason I remember touching home is because I had to get through 25 guys to get there."

Q How many times did Max Carey, the National League record holder, steal home during his career?

A 33. Ty Cobb holds the major league mark with 50. Honus Wagner ranks fourth with 27, one behind long-time New York Giants outfielder George Burns.

Q Which Olympic champion served as the main speaker at groundbreaking ceremonies for Three Rivers Stadium on April 25, 1968?

A Jesse Owens, a four-time gold medalist (long jump, 100 meters, 200 meters, 400-meter relay) at the 1936 Games in Berlin.

Q Which Pirate drew a 15-day suspension and a $5,000 fine—one of the most serious penalties ever handed down—for a run-in with an umpire?

A Third baseman Bill Madlock, who poked plate umpire Gerry Crawford in the nose with his glove while gesturing during a May 1, 1980, game against Montreal at Three Rivers Stadium. The National League responded with the harshest reprimand ever for an on-field incident.

Madlock had been called out on strikes with the bases loaded to end the fifth inning. He argued with Crawford at the plate and then made his costly gesture after a teammate brought him his mitt.

"There was no intent on my part," Madlock explained. "If I wanted to hit the man, I could have hit him. I pushed the glove near his face. There was no intent to hurt him."

When league president Chub Feeney did not issue an immediate ruling—he expressed a need to review film of the altercation—umpire John Kibler's crew vowed to boycott the May 2 game at Three Rivers. Pirates manager Chuck Tanner, acting as an intermediary, talked the umpires out of such a rash act, but Kibler still was livid.

"Films! What does he need films for? He just has to look in the newspapers and see [photos of] Madlock hitting Crawford," Kibler fumed. "What about us? What about the safety of the umpires? Suppose Madlock gets angry again and comes at one of us with a bat?"

Feeney finally handed down his ruling on June 2. Madlock filed an immediate appeal but then reconsidered after a chat with Pirates owner John Galbreath. He withdrew the appeal and began serving his sentence on June 6.

Madlock's defenders denounced the penalty as excessive, especially in the context of history. They cited the Juan Marichal case. After clubbing Dodgers catcher John Roseboro over the head with a bat at home plate during a 1965 game, the San Francisco pitcher was fined $1,750 and suspended for eight days.

142

Ironically, Feeney was the Giants' vice president back then. And the plate umpire? Gerry Crawford's father, Shag.

Q Forbes Field was razed in the 1970s, but a small section of the red-brick wall over which Bill Mazeroski's championship-winning home run flew in 1960 still stands. Where?

A It was reconstructed, brick by brick, in the Allegheny Club at Three Rivers Stadium.

Q Where did home plate wind up after Forbes Field was torn down?

A It's enclosed in glass on a first-floor walkway at the University of Pittsburgh's Forbes Quadrangle. The rubber slab rests in almost exactly the same position it did in 1970. To place the plate in precisely the same position would have necessitated locating it inside a women's restroom.

The only other indication that a ballpark once stood on the site is a section of the left field wall and the flagpole, situated across the street from the Quadrangle.

Q Roberto Clemente appeared in 14 World Series games during his career. In how many of those games did he hit safely?

A All 14. Clemente collected 21 hits and batted .362 in the 1960 and 1971 Series.

Yankees outfielder Hank Bauer holds the Series record for the longest batting streak: 17 games, spanning the 1956, 1957 and 1958 Fall Classics.

FIRE ALARM

P irates pitcher Marty O'Toole was forced to leave a 1912 game against Philadelphia for an unusual reason—an inflamed tongue, the result of some mischief perpetrated by the Phillies.

O'Toole, whose repertoire was limited to spitballs, disgusted opponents with a distasteful pre-pitch routine. He would hide the ball in his glove, bring it to his face and then lick it. Philadelphia first baseman Fred Luderus countered this offensive practice one day by stashing a tube of liniment in his pocket and smearing some on the ball at every opportunity (back then, a single baseball might stay in play for several innings).

Before long, O'Toole's distress was so profound he had to exit the game. Pittsburgh manager Fred Clarke approached the umpires and protested Luderas' actions, but Phils manager Red Dooin insisted the liniment was simply a safeguard.

"That ball may be carrying the germs of any one of many contagious diseases," he explained. "So we put disinfectant on it whenever we face a spitball pitcher like O'Toole. I do not see how we can be refused the privilege of protecting ourselves."

The umpires agreed.

Q Which two Pirates knocked in 100 or more runs a team-record five consecutive seasons?

A Pie Traynor (1927-31) and Ralph Kiner (1947-51). Traynor reached the century mark seven times in his career, matching Honus Wagner's team record.

Q Which Pirate shares the major league record for most stolen bases in a World Series game?

A Honus Wagner, who swiped three bases against Detroit in Game 3 on Oct. 11, 1909, leading Pittsburgh to an 8-6 victory. "Wagner plays rings around Tyrus Cobb," read a subhead in the next day's *Pittsburg Press*.

Wagner went 3-for-5 with three RBIs to pace the Pirates' attack and overshadow Cobb, the Tigers' top player. He stole second base in the first, second and fifth innings.

"It was Wagner's Day, with an uppercase W and a capital D," *The New York Times* pointed out. "The Flying Dutchman had on his hitting clothes, and he also had rubbed mercury on his feet for the occasion."

Wagner held sole possession of the stolen base record for 56 years until Willie Davis of the Dodgers pilfered three against Minnesota in Game 5 of the 1965 World Series. Lou Brock equaled the record during both the 1967 and 1968 Series.

Q What was located under the left field bleachers at Forbes Field during the 1920s?

A A Studebaker dealership and a car-repair shop.

Q This Pirate made his major league debut in 1970 under manager Danny Murtaugh, his father's Philadelphia Phillies teammate for three seasons. Name him.

A Catcher Milt May. Third baseman Merrill "Pinky" May was Murtaugh's infield mate from 1941 to 1943.

Q This player is, quite possibly, the only Pirate to slug two home runs in his first game with the team, a feat that sparked a thunderous standing ovation—and a curtain call in response. Name him.

A Veteran shortstop Shawon Dunston, who debuted with the Bucs on Sept. 2, 1997, against Cleveland at Three Rivers Stadium. Dunston hammered a solo home run in his first at bat and then delivered a three-run shot in the sixth, wiping out a 3-2 deficit and propelling Pittsburgh to a 6-4 victory before 43,380 fans.

"That was good to see," said outfielder Al Martin after Dunston twice victimized the Indians' Jaret Wright. "There's no better way to get your teammates believing in you than to do something dramatic like he did."

Dunston was acquired from the Cubs in exchange for a minor-league prospect after injuries to Kevin Elster and Kevin Polcovich left the Bucs without a veteran shortstop in the midst of a pennant race. He hit .394 and slugged five home runs in 18 games for the Pirates in September.

Q Who was the last Pirate—maybe the first, too—to sing the national anthem before a game in Pittsburgh?

A Pitcher Manny Sarmiento, a native of Venezuela. Sarmiento did the honors on Oct. 3, 1982, and again on July 4, 1983.

Q Who was the first Pirate to hit home runs from both sides of the plate in the same game?

A Bobby Bonilla. He victimized the Dodgers' Fernando Valenzuela from the right side in the third inning and then homered left-handed off Ken Howell in the seventh inning of a 6-0 victory on July 3, 1987, at Three Rivers Stadium.

That Fourth of July-eve display of pyrotechnics was notable in that players homering both right-handed and left-handed in the same game occurs so infrequently. Even no-hitters are more common.

Bonilla duplicated his feat on April 6, 1988, against the Phillies. Dale Sveum became only the second Pirate to connect from both sides in the same game against Cincinnati on Aug. 18, 1999.

Q Which non-uniformed Pirates employee received a tongue-in-cheek vote in the 1960 National League MVP balloting?

A Team groundskeeper Eddie Dunn, who maintained a lightning-fast infield at Forbes Field, a real boon to Buc batters. George Kiseda of the *Philadelphia Daily News*—formerly a member of the *Pittsburgh Sun-Telegraph* staff—figured Dunn's handiwork merited an MVP vote.

Q What nickname did critics bestow on Dunn's rock-hard infield?

A The alabaster plaster. Even the Pirates made light of Forbes Field's concrete-like surface. During the 1959 season, Bucs first baseman Ted Kluszewski sidled up to Dunn, needle poised. "Hey, Eddie," he said, "I have a friend who would like to borrow your infield formula. He's building highways over in Ohio."

ROYAL TREATMENT

O ne of the oddest episodes in Pirates history occurred in 1975 when Pittsburgh honored broadcasters Bob Prince and Nellie King—after they were *fired*. The tribute featured a downtown parade.

It was hardly a typical response. Then again, there was nothing typical about the Bucs' broadcast team. Prince and King endeared themselves to their listeners, who regarded them as royalty in more than name only. When they were dismissed following the season, the public outcry—outrage, even—ran deeper than anyone at Westinghouse Broadcasting Co., owner of KDKA, the Bucs' flagship station, could have imagined.

"They made a decision in their ivory tower and it blew up in their face," said Jack Wheeler of Pittsburgh radio station WEEP, which promoted the Nov. 5 parade. "They misread the pulse of the public."

That was evident by the overwhelming response. The firing triggered an avalanche of letters and calls of protest. Switchboards lit up at Pirates headquarters and at KDKA. Even Vera Clemente, Roberto's widow, called from Puerto Rico.

Fans were stunned by the news, as were many of the players. "Bob's a landmark," said Willie Stargell. "It's like the U.S. Steel building falling down."

The always-partisan Prince joined the Pittsburgh broadcast team in 1948 and had been the voice of the Pirates since 1955. King had just wrapped up his ninth season as Prince's sidekick. According to Edward Wallis, regional vice president of Westinghouse Broadcasting, their work had suffered in recent months.

"The very nature of our business is constantly changing and over the last couple years we had realized that our presentation of baseball also had to change," he said. When Prince was reluctant to do so, Wallis dropped the ax. King was a collateral casualty.

If Wallis expected the tempest to blow over quickly, he made a colossal miscalculation. Even Bill Currie, a sportscaster at KDKA-TV, rose to the defense of Prince and King.

"The dismissal of Bob and Nellie is no longer an internal company matter, but a matter of supreme public interest," Currie said in a KDKA commentary. "Prince has his critics and detractors, but he has no known enemies and his long tenure makes him Mr. Baseball here. His hundreds of acts of charity have elevated him to a place of public esteem, where nobody can kiss him off with a terse statement on one day's notice and expect public understanding."

Phil Musick of the *Pittsburgh Press* penned a touching tribute to the man whose voice "always sounded like he'd been gargling with emery boards." Wrote Musick, "For a long, long time in this town, baseball will remain a guy with a razorish voice, an Adam's apple you could cut paper with and a way of saying 'We had 'em all the way' that made you wonder what time the next day's game began."

There would be no next game for Prince and King, so Pittsburgh threw them a going-away party. They stood atop a fire truck as the parade snaked its way from the Civic Arena to the Hilton Hotel, Prince waving a foot-long Green Weenie like a scepter. The tribute continued with a rally at Point State Park, attended by Pirates, politicians and fans. Ten thousand of them.

The outpouring of support overwhelmed Prince and King. For Prince, the parade and rally put a positive spin on an otherwise excruciating experience.

"I'm glad I didn't have to die," he said, "to find out how people really feel about me."

Q Who succeeded Prince as voice of the Pirates?

A Milo Hamilton, who had himself been fired in 1975 by the Atlanta Braves.

"I would hope this doesn't sound too egotistical," said Prince in the wake of his dismissal, "but I would think the man who has to follow me is going to have some problems for awhile."

Prince was prescient on that count: Hamilton never did gain the acceptance of Pittsburgh fans and departed after four seasons. He now broadcasts Houston Astros games.

Q What World Series record did Pirates pitcher Kent Tekulve set in 1979?

A Most saves in a Series, with three. Of course, there's a figurative asterisk beside Tekulve's name—he actually *tied* the record.

One of his Pirates predecessors, Elroy Face, was credited with three saves in the 1960 Series, the first pitcher to do so. But at that time, saves were not recognized as an official statistic.

Tekulve's record finally fell in 1996, when John Wetteland of the Yankees saved all four New York victories over Atlanta.

Q Which pitcher served up Roberto Clemente's 3,000th career hit?

A Jon Matlack of the Mets. Clemente became the 11th member of the 3,000-hit club on Sept. 30, 1972, drilling a fourth-inning double to the left-center wall at Three Rivers Stadium. It was his last regular-season hit.

Q Who replaced Honus Wagner as the Pirates' shortstop?

A Rookie Chuck Ward, who debuted in 1917 when Wagner was shifted to first base. Ward batted a disappointing .236, made 52 errors and was dealt to Brooklyn after the season. He never played as a regular again.

Q Which two Pirates went on the vaudeville circuit and shared a stage with Jack Benny after leading the team to the National League title?

A The Waners, Paul and Lloyd. Following the 1927 season, the brothers sought to capitalize on their newfound popularity as players by going into show business. Clad in Pirates uniforms, Paul played the saxophone and Lloyd the violin. Benny served as their emcee. The Waners earned upwards of $2,000 a week, which exceeded what they received for playing baseball.

Q Lou Brock of the Cardinals once refused to bat against Pirates pitcher Bob Veale. Why?

A Fear. Veale threw as hard as any major league hurler in the mid-1960s and his control was iffy, so batters—especially left-handed batters like

Brock—swallowed hard before stepping in against the Pittsburgh southpaw. Brock was especially reluctant one steamy night at Forbes Field.

"Bob sweated profusely—the sweat would run down on his glasses and sometimes they'd fog up," recalled ex-Pirates pitcher Nellie Briles, Brock's teammate at the time. "It kept happening to him this one night. He would wipe off his glasses, they would fog up in no time and he'd stop to wipe them. He finally got tired of it, took off his glasses and put them in his pocket. He decided to pitch without them."

At that point, Brock stepped out and refused to re-enter the batter's box. Veale was intimidating enough when he *could* see the plate. But without his glasses? Brock stood his ground.

Veale finally relented. He put on his glasses and play resumed.

Q Which future Pirate saved himself $20 in the minors by catching a *bat*?

A Danny Murtaugh, who was playing for Houston of the Texas League in the early 1940s when he took a 3-2 pitch for a third strike. Angered, he tossed his bat high in the air. "If that bat lands," barked the plate umpire, "I'm fining you $20." Murtaugh settled under the descending bat and made a money-saving catch.

Q Speaking of strange catches—which Pirate once "caught" his own home run ball?

A Dixie Walker, who went deep against the Dodgers in a 1949 game at Brooklyn's Ebbets Field.

After the Pirates were retired, Walker trotted out to his right field position and glanced up at the ball he'd hit—it was stuck in the screen above the wall. Walker strolled over, gave the screen a good yank and the ball popped loose. It dropped right into his glove.

A WINNING DIRECTOR

J immy Long unexpectedly helped the Pirates win a game during the 1948 season—without even touching a bat or a ball.

Fact is, Long wasn't even in the lineup. His position with the Bucs? Director of publicity.

The alert Long, a former newspaperman, detected something amiss during an Aug. 25 game against Brooklyn that escaped the notice of even the umpires. Without his intervention, the Pirates would have lost. In fact, they *did* lose.

Pittsburgh trailed 11-9 with two outs in the bottom of the ninth at Forbes Field. When consecutive batters reached base, Dodgers manager Burt Shotton replaced pitcher Hugh Casey with rookie Carl Erskine, who promptly went to a 3-1 count on Eddie Bockman. Shotton trudged back to the mound and summoned Hank Behrman, who retired Bockman with his first pitch to end the game.

Or so everyone thought. Everyone, that is, but Long, who realized the Dodgers had violated a rule: Barring injury, a relief pitcher has to face at least one batter before leaving the mound. He called the oversight to the attention of the sportswriters covering the game, who relayed the information to Pirates manager Billy Meyer. Meyer filed an immediate protest.

National League president Ford Frick upheld the protest a day later and the game was resumed Sept. 21 from the point where Erskine illegally departed. It ended in six minutes' time. Erskine walked Bockman, loading the bases for Stan Rojek, who ripped a three-run double off Behrman to wrap up an unusual 12-11 victory.

Wrote Vince Johnson of the *Pittsburgh Post-Gazette,* "It is probably the first time in the history of baseball that a publicity man put a game in the win column."

Q This former Pirate earned a place in baseball history by becoming the first player to produce 30-homer seasons in two leagues. Name him.

A First baseman Dick Stuart, who slugged 35 homers for the Pirates in 1961 and hit 42 with the Red Sox in 1963. More than a dozen players have since joined the club, including another Pirates first baseman: Jason Thompson, who smacked 31 homers for the Tigers in 1977 and 31 for the Bucs in 1982.

Q In 1971, the Pirates won the World Series against a Baltimore team that featured four 20-game winners. Name them.

A Dave McNally (21-5), Pat Dobson (20-8), Mike Cuellar (20-9) and Jim Palmer (20-9). The only other major league team to produce four 20-game winners was the 1920 White Sox, who failed to win the pennant.

Q Name the only player in the Pirates' all-time top 10 in home runs who never hit at least 20 in a given season.

A Bill Mazeroski, who ranks seventh with 138 career homers. Maz clubbed 19 in his best season, 1958.

Q Breaking his own team record was a painful experience for Pirates catcher Jason Kendall in 1997. What did he do to earn a place in the record book?

A Kendall was hit by pitches 31 times, easily surpassing his standard of 15 set as a rookie in 1996. He finished second in the majors in that category to Craig Biggio of Houston, who was plunked 34 times.

Kendall then tied his mark while leading the majors in 1998, becoming the first big leaguer in the modern era with two seasons of 30-plus, much less two in succession. He's on a pace to shatter the all-time big league mark of 260, held by Hall of Famer Hughie Jennings (1891-1912).

"I hope I don't get the record," said Kendall during the 1998 season. "I mean, it hurts. My left arm is pretty much black and blue for six months."

The single-season big league record is 50, set by Montreal's Ron Hunt in 1971.

Q Who was the Pirates' last player-manager?

A Billy Herman, who appeared in 15 games, mostly at second base, for the 1947 Bucs. Herman, acquired from the Braves in an offseason trade, managed the team to a 61-92 record before he was relieved of his duties with one game remaining.

Q Who holds the Pirates record for highest batting average in a season?

A Arky Vaughan, with a league-leading .385 figure in 1935, the best ever by a National League shortstop in the modern era. Vaughan never hit below .300 in his 10 seasons (1932-41) with the Bucs and finished his 14-year career with a .318 average.

Honus Wagner (.381 in 1900) and Paul Waner (.380 in 1927) rank second and third on the club's all-time list. Roberto Clemente posted the highest average in the post-World War II era, hitting .357 in 1967 en route to his fourth and final batting crown.

Remarkably, only two shortstops have posted higher single-season averages than Vaughan: Hall of Famer Hughie Jennings of Baltimore (.386 in 1895 and .401 in 1896) and Luke Appling of the White Sox (.388 in 1936).

Q How many Pirates hit at least 20 home runs in a season during the first 50 years of the franchise's existence?

A None. It wasn't until 1938—the team's 52nd season—that Johnny Rizzo slugged 23. As late as 1924—three years after Babe Ruth hit 59 homers for the Yankees—the club record was a modest 13, set by Jake Stenzel back in 1894.

Q The last player to homer over the right field roof at Forbes Field was also the first to hit an upper deck home run at Three Rivers Stadium. Name him.

A Willie Stargell, who hit his seventh roof-clearing blast at Forbes Field—the 18th overall—on April 25, 1970, off Hoyt Wilhelm of Atlanta. Stargell then launched a delivery from Ron Taylor of the Mets into the right field upper deck at Three Rivers on Aug. 9, 1970. No other player reached the roof at Forbes Field or the upper deck at Three Rivers Stadium (four times) as often as Stargell.

A FOND FAREWELL

When the Pirates hired Jim Leyland in November of 1985, one newspaper "welcomed" the new manager with a two-word headline: "Jim who?" Eleven years later there was no question about his identity—or his hold on the hearts of a city.

Leyland's arrival in Pittsburgh might have elicited a figurative shrug of the shoulders, but his departure was accompanied by an outpouring of emotion the likes of which has rarely been seen at Three Rivers Stadium.

More than 20,000 fans turned out on Sept. 25, 1996, for Leyland's final home appearance as the Pirates' manager. They helped transform an otherwise meaningless, late-season, midweek game against the Cardinals into something magical. The fans gave their departing manager—he would soon sign with the Florida Marlins—a rousing sendoff that featured cheers and tears and a video salute from President Bill Clinton.

It wasn't a game, it was a lovefest. The fans stood and applauded Leyland's every appearance, even when he strolled to the mound to change pitchers. Afterwards, Leyland embraced St. Louis manager Tony La Russa, who gave him his first major league job as a White Sox coach in 1982, and wept on his shoulder as the cheers continued, unabated.

"I don't know if any of us will ever see anything like this again," said La Russa. "It was like the Cal Ripken game. You had to be here to really believe it."

The fans stayed to the end of the three-hour, 43-minute marathon—St. Louis won 8-7 in 11 innings—and showered Leyland with applause as he waved his cap in acknowledgement.

"I know exactly how the fans feel," said shortstop Jay Bell. "It just shows you how much people here love and respect Jim. He's given his heart and soul to this community. I think we all finally realize how much Jim means to the city of Pittsburgh."

Leyland was hired following a season tainted by 104 defeats and a drug scandal that gave the Pirates—and the city—a black eye. He restored pride and dignity to the team and led the Bucs to three division titles. In the process, the native of Perrysburg, Ohio, was adopted by Pittsburghers as one of their own.

"You reached out to take my hand on my first day here and you captured my heart not long after that," he told listeners on his pre-game radio show. "I'll be indebted to this city the rest of my life."

Q Which Pirate became the first major leaguer to steal home twice in a game?

A Honus Wagner, who pilfered the plate in the first and third innings of a 7-0 win over the Giants at New York's Polo Grounds on June 20, 1901. He went 4-for-5 and stole three bases all told.

"The stout but agile Wagner performed conspicuously," noted an account in the *Pittsburg Post*. "He made four hits and two runs and skipped around the bases with all the abandon of a child playing crack the whip. He was as care free, once he got to first base, as a bull calf in a ten-acre lot, taking part in two 'double' steals, which landed him at the plate."

Not only was Wagner a daring baserunner; he possessed deceptive speed. Said his contemporary, Hall of Fame outfielder Sam Crawford, "He looked so awkward—bowlegged, barrel-chested, about 200 pounds, a big man. And yet he could run like a scared rabbit."

Wagner utilized that speed to lead the league in stolen bases on five occasions between 1901 and 1908, averaging 52 per season over that span.

Only 10 other big leaguers have swiped home twice in a game, the most recent being Cleveland's Vic Power in 1958.

Q Like television's Everready bunny, this Pirates pitcher just kept going and going and going—right into the record book. He established a major league mark—since surpassed—by appearing in nine consecutive games. Name him.

A Elroy Face, who took part in every Pirates game between Sept. 3 and Sept. 13, 1956. Face led the majors in appearances that year with 68.

Mike Marshall of the Dodgers set the existing consecutive game mark of 13 in 1974 and Dale Mohorcic of Texas tied it in 1986. Face still holds the Pirates' record.

Q Which Pirate holds the major league record for most consecutive games with at least one extra-base hit?

A Paul Waner, who collected extra-base hits in an astounding 14 consecutive games from June 3 through June 19, 1927. During his torrid tear, Waner smacked 20 extra-base hits (12 doubles, four triples, four home runs), batted .525 (32-for-61) and had an astronomical 1.049 slugging percentage.

Q This future Pirate celebrated a no-hitter in 1973, the same year his brother celebrated an NBA championship. Name him.

A Jim Bibby, who was pitching for Texas when he no-hit Oakland on July 20. Only weeks before, brother Henry wrapped up his rookie year as a pro by helping the New York Knicks win an NBA title.

Jim Bibby experienced the euphoria of a world championship with the Pirates in 1979, contributing a 12-4 record. A year later he finished 19-6 to lead the league in winning percentage (.760).

That was a modest percentage compared to UCLA's during Henry's three varsity seasons as a starting guard under John Wooden. The Bruins compiled an 87-3 (.967) record while rolling to three NCAA championships.

Jim Bibby is now a pitching coach with the Pirates' Carolina League farm club in Lynchburg, Va. Henry Bibby coaches basketball at Southern Cal, his alma mater's crosstown rival.

Q Who led the 1960 Pirates in RBIs?

A Roberto Clemente, with 94. That's one reason Clemente was miffed when he finished only eighth in the National League MVP voting.

Q Did the largest baseball crowd in Pittsburgh history witness a Pirates victory or a Pirates defeat?

A Neither. A record throng of 59,568 squeezed into Three Rivers Stadium on July 12, 1994, for the major league All-Star game, won 8-7 by the National League in 10 innings.

The next five largest crowds in Three Rivers Stadium history occurred during National League Championship Series games against the Atlanta Braves in 1991 and 1992. The regular-season record was set on April 8, 1991, when the Bucs lost their home opener to Montreal before 54,274 fans.

An overflow throng of 44,932 filed into Forbes Field on Sept. 23, 1956, for a game against Brooklyn, setting that ballpark's single-game attendance record. The attraction was Prize Day, as fan appreciation day was known. The size of the crowd is notable in that Forbes Field's official capacity that season was listed as 34,249.

Q Name the only Pirate to also play for the Steelers.

A Rex Johnston, a two-sport standout at the University of Southern California. Johnston saw limited action, mostly on special teams, for the 1960 Steelers and then returned to Pittsburgh four years later, appearing in 14 games as an outfielder with the Bucs. He was hitless in seven trips to the plate.

Johnston earned five letters at USC, three as a halfback (1956-58) and two as an outfielder (1958-59). The Trojans' 1958 baseball squad, led by four future major leaguers—Johnston, Don Buford, Ron Fairly and Len Gabrielson—won the College World Series with an 8-7 victory over Missouri. Johnston scored the deciding run in the 12th inning.

He never experienced such thrills in the big leagues. Johnston's abbreviated stay in Pittsburgh in 1964 lasted only until the end of April, when teams' expanded rosters had to be pared to 25.

"It was between me and Manny Mota," he recalled. "Manny had a terrible month and was going down the next day. They even told me to get an apartment. Then, on the last day of the month, Manny went 4-for-4. They sent me out instead."

Consequently, Johnston's career lasted less than a month. Mota's lasted 20 years.

One for the Ages

Catcher Bill Farmer and pitcher Babe Adams represent polar opposites among the 1,500 or so names listed on Pittsburgh's all-time roster. They are, respectively, the youngest and oldest players to wear a Pirates uniform.

Farmer was 17 years, four months, four days old on May 1, 1888, when he debuted in a 10-1 loss at Detroit. According to a *Pittsburgh Post* account, "Farmer, the new catcher, did fairly well, but was nervous."

No surprise, given his age. Farmer went hitless at the plate and committed two errors behind it. He appeared in only four more big league games and was out of the majors by the end of the year. Farmer batted .125 in his brief career.

Pitchers Bill Bishop and Andy Dunning rank second and third in terms of youth. Bishop was 17 years, four months, 13 days of age on May 9, 1887, when he allowed 16 hits and five walks, uncorked three wild pitches and hit a batter in a 10-3 loss to the eventual NL champion Detroit Wolverines. He finished his career not long after that, saddled with an 0-4 record and a 9.96 ERA.

Dunning likewise flamed out quickly. He compiled an 0-3 record after making his debut on May 23, 1889, at the age of 17 years, nine months, 11 days.

Catcher Nick Koback, who debuted 10 days after his 18th birthday on July 29, 1953, holds the distinction of being the youngest Pirate in the modern era. Koback went 0-for-2 after entering in the sixth inning of an 8-2 loss at St. Louis. He appeared in 16 games for the Bucs over a three-year span, hitting .121.

At the opposite end of the spectrum, Adams was 44 years, two months, 24 days of age when he hurled two-thirds of an inning in relief during a 4-2 loss at Brooklyn on Aug. 11, 1926. He was given his unconditional release two days later.

Diomedes Olivo and Honus Wagner rank right behind Adams. Olivo was 43 years, eight months, eight days old when he pitched four innings in the Bucs' season finale against Milwaukee on Sept. 30, 1962. Wagner was 43 years, six months, 24 days of age when he made his final appearance on Sept. 17, 1917, as a late-innings defensive replacement at second base in a game against Boston.

Q Although he was christened Maximilian Carnarius, this Pirates Hall of Famer is better known by another name. What?

A Max Carey. The fleet outfielder spent parts of 17 seasons (1910-26) with the Bucs.

Q The Pirates' game against the New York Giants on June 18, 1941, was held up 56 minutes. By what?

A A boxing match. Pittsburgh's Billy Conn battled defending champion Joe Louis that night in a heavyweight title bout at New York's Polo Grounds. In what John Drebinger of *The New York Times* called "an extraordinary double feature," the baseball game was halted after the Giants batted in the fourth inning so the 24,378 fans at Forbes Field could listen to a broadcast of the bout over the ballpark's loudspeakers.

The Pittsburgh Kid, as Conn was known, fought several times at Forbes Field during his career, including a tuneup for the showdown with Louis. He was leading on points after 12 rounds, then made the mistake of going for a knockout in the 13th. Louis took advantage of an opening, delivered a telling blow and dropped Conn to the canvas.

The Pirates and Giants then resumed the baseball game, but unlike the fight, there was no winner. The teams were locked in a 2-2 tie after 11 innings when they were forced to stop again—this time by the major league curfew.

Q What are the four stages of senility, according to former Pirates general manager Branch Rickey?

A In his own words, "First you forget names. Then you forget faces. Then you forget to zip up your fly. Then you forget to zip *down* your fly."

Q Who was the highest-paid member of the 1960 Pirates? (And care to venture a guess as to his salary?)

A Pitcher Bob Friend, who'd been with the Bucs since 1951. Friend earned $42,500 in 1960, edging out pitcher Vernon Law ($40,000), another long-time Pirate. World Series hero Bill Mazeroski was paid only $17,500, National League MVP and batting champion Dick Groat made $18,500 and future Hall of Famer Roberto Clemente earned $25,000.

"Being paid was a bonus for us," said Groat years later. "We all made a good living and stayed young playing a kid's game. What more could we ask?"

"I think we all felt that way," said Mazeroski. "I knew I never was going to be rich, but I had enough to eat and enough to keep my fishing hooks baited. That's all I cared about."

Of course, many members of the 1960 Bucs cringe when they consider the megabuck salaries prevalent today. There are dozens of current players who earn more in a single day than any of the Pirates did for their entire world championship season.

"I was born 30 years too soon," lamented relief pitcher Elroy Face. "But I can't do anything to change that, so why worry about it?"

Q Salaries have skyrocketed since 1960, even in small-market Pittsburgh. Case in point: the contract extension signed by Kevin Young on March 6, 1999, the richest pact in franchise history. How much will Young earn over the life of the contract?

A $24 million. The 29-year-old first baseman, who led the Bucs with 27 home runs and 108 RBIs in 1998, will make $2 million in 1999 before his new four-year deal kicks in next season. Young will receive $5.5 million in 2000, $6 million in 2001, $5.5 million in 2002 and $6.5 million in 2003. A $500,000 signing bonus was part of the package.

The irony is that Young was once viewed as expendable by the Pirates, who released him in March of 1996. He signed with Kansas City, but suffered another blow when the Royals cut him loose at the close of the season. Young's fortunes finally turned around after he re-signed with the Bucs in December. He started the 1997 season on the bench, but by June he had earned a starting position. The one-time castoff has been an integral part of the team ever since.

"It's an unbelievable story," Young said. "It's almost like a storybook the way this all worked out."

Shortstop Jay Bell held the previous team record for the richest contract, a $17.5 million, four-year deal signed in 1993.

Q Who were the Black Maxers?

A Members of a club founded by Pirates pitcher Steve Blass during the 1966 season to help keep the team loose in the pressure-cooker atmosphere of a pennant race.

Blass was inspired to create the Black Maxers—there were 12 charter members—after watching a film about World War I flying aces.

"It was designed out of a boring day in Chicago when I saw *The Blue Max*, with George Peppard," Blass recalled. "I scoured the novelty shops and bought a few items."

Such as black crosses, patterned on those featured in the movie. Blass awarded them to teammates for dubious achievements, such as striking out with the bases loaded.

The Black Maxers and their oddball presentations provided comic relief for a collection of players who were flaky to begin with. And proud of it. "We haven't got a sane guy on the club," crowed catcher Jim Pagliaroni. Wrote Leonard Koppett of *The New York Times*, "The Pirates may not win the pennant, but whatever stops them, it will not be the weight of solemnity."

Pittsburgh occupied first place for extended stretches of the 1966 season before finishing third, only three games behind the champion Dodgers.

Q Pittsburgh mayor David L. Lawrence fined the Pirates $100 on May 10, 1948. Why?

A The Bucs had violated a 7 p.m. Sunday curfew mandated by Pennsylvania's Blue Laws the day before by continuing a twinbill with Brooklyn until the final out was recorded at 7:40.

"The Pirates may not have made baseball history when they split a doubleheader with the Dodgers Sunday, but they may have made history of another sort," wrote Vince Johnson of the *Pittsburgh Post-Gazette*. "Shortly before 7 p.m., a public address announcement advised the overflow crowd of 40,797 that play would continue until 8 p.m. The customers, some of whom already had started for the exits, returned to their seats."

General manager Ray Hamey ordered the second game to continue based on his erroneous interpretation of the Blue Laws. He believed the curfew could be extended one hour when Daylight Savings Time was in effect. "It was an honest mistake," Hamey said in his defense.

But Lawrence didn't buy Hamey's explanation. Acting on the advice of the City Law Department, he docked the Pirates.

The doubleheader ran long because pitchers from both clubs struggled to retire batters. Brooklyn won the first game by a 14-2 score before Pittsburgh rebounded to take the nightcap 10-8 on the strength of Ralph Kiner's two home runs and five RBIs.

Q In a malaprop worthy of Yogi Berra, Pirates pitching coach Pete Vuckovich gave a curious explanation for his ejection from a 1997 game at St. Louis. What did he say?

A After umpire Randy Marsh gave him the heave-ho, Vuckovich told the press that "I was a victim of circumcision."

THE LONGEST WALK

When the Pirates bolted into a 10-0 first-inning lead at Philadelphia on June 8, 1989, giddiness overwhelmed broadcaster Jim Rooker. If the Bucs lose this one, he told listeners, I'll walk back to Pittsburgh.

Nine innings later the Phillies were celebrating an improbable 15-11 victory and Rooker was mapping out a route west.

The Pirates utilized eight hits and five walks in the first, the key blow a three-run homer by Barry Bonds. But not even a 10-run lead was secure the way Pittsburgh's pitchers were serving up gopher balls. Light-hitting shortstop Steve Jeltz slugged two- and three-run homers, Von Hayes smashed a pair of two-run homers and Darren Daulton delivered a two-run single off reliever Jeff Robinson that snapped an 11-11 eighth-inning tie.

"I don't know if I can put it into words, except to say it was the absolute worst," said Robinson, who allowed four runs in one-third of an inning and was saddled with the loss. "It just couldn't get any worse than that."

Rooker made good on his promise after the season, hoofing it from Philadelphia to Pittsburgh while collecting donations for charitable causes. His feet were a mass of blisters during the 12-day trek.

"It was 315 miles, which for me was 314 too many," said Rooker. "The upside was that we raised $81,000 for charity."

Q How many times have the Pirates led the National League in home attendance?

A Just twice, in 1925 and 1948. The pennant-winning Pirates drew a team-record 804,354 fans in 1925, beating out New York (778,993) for top honors. The fourth-place 1948 club played before 1,517,021 fans, just ahead of New York (1,459,269).

Since the formation of the American League in 1901, the Bucs have finished no higher than third—in 1926, 1927 and 1960—among all major league teams.

Q What modern National League record did Roberto Clemente set in 1970—after receiving a goat milk rubdown from trainer Tony Bartirome?

A He pounded out 10 hits in consecutive games.

Clemente's chronically aching back was particularly bothersome prior to an Aug. 22 game at Los Angeles, so he asked Bartirome to try the unorthodox treatment. Clemente responded with a 5-for-7 performance at the plate and scored the deciding run in a 16-inning 2-1 victory.

Convinced of the therapeutic value of his milky rubdown, Clemente requested another before the next day's game. He went 5-for-6 with a home run, scored four times and knocked in three runs as the Bucs breezed to an 11-0 win.

"Ten hits in two games," marveled manager Danny Murtaugh. "Man, when I was playing it'd take me three or four weeks to get that many."

Clemente hit a sizzling .352 for the season, although a variety of physical ailments limited him to 108 games. Especially troublesome was his back, which had plagued him off and on since 1954, when a drunk driver rammed his car in Puerto Rico.

Said Clemente, "My back hurts me when I sit down. It hurts me when I stand up. It hurts me even when I breathe sometimes."

Yet Clemente seemed the picture of health on Aug. 22 and 23 when his assault on the Dodgers' pitching staff threatened a 94-year-old major league record. The all-time mark of 12 hits in consecutive games was set in 1876 by Cal McVey of the Chicago White Stockings. Cleveland's Johnny Burnett established the modern record of 11 hits in 1932.

Q Which current Pirate holds the major league record for most hits in three consecutive games?

A Mike Benjamin, who went 14-for-18 during a torrid stretch for San Francisco in 1995. The journeyman infielder, a .186 career batter entering that season, was filling in for injured third baseman Matt Williams.

"In the role I'm in, you don't think a whole lot of records are realistic," he said at the time. "The guys who play every day have the best chance of accomplishing them."

With Williams watching from the bench, Benjamin made the most of his starting opportunity. He went 4-for-6 in a 13-inning loss to Montreal on June 11 and followed with a 4-for-5 performance in an 8-4 victory over Chicago on June 13. He then tied a franchise record with six hits in seven at bats and equaled Clemente's mark of 10 hits in consecutive games during a 4-3 win over the Cubs on June 14. Benjamin's single in the top of the 13th brought home the deciding run and enabled him to surpass the old record of 13 hits in three games shared by Hall of Famer Joe Cronin of Washington (1933), Detroit's Walt Dropo (1952) and Tim Salmon of California (1994).

Said San Francisco manager Dusty Baker, "I've been around some great hitters—[Hank] Aaron, [Orlando] Cepeda, Ralph Garr, Rico Carty, Steve Garvey, Reggie Smith—but I've never seen a finer three days than he's had."

Discounting his 14-for-18 outburst, Benjamin hit .161 for the season. But for three games, at least, he swung the bat like someone destined for Cooperstown.

"It actually seemed easy," said Benjamin, who was acquired by the Pirates from Boston on Nov. 17, 1998. "I wasn't thinking about anything other than, if it's over the plate, I'm going to get a hit. It was like everything was in slow motion. It was weird."

Q Name the most recent Pirates employee to win a major individual honor.

A General manager Cam Bonifay, who was selected as *The Sporting News* Executive of the Year in 1997. The low-budget Pirates, despite a payroll that barely exceeded the individual salaries of the majors' megastars, stunned baseball by challenging for the Central Division title right down to the final week of the season.

General manager Joe L. Brown was the only other team executive to claim top honors (1958). The award was inaugurated in 1936 when *The Sporting News* honored Cardinals GM Branch Rickey—who later served in the same capacity in Pittsburgh—for the first of three times.

Q Who drew blood to help the Pirates score a World Series insurance run?

A Trainer Tony Bartirome. The Bucs led 3-1 in the ninth inning of Game 7 in 1979 when Bill Robinson, batting with the bases loaded, tried to elude an inside pitch from Dennis Martinez and went spinning. Bartirome raced from the dugout to check on Robinson.

"It didn't hit me," he whispered to Bartirome.

"The hell it didn't," said Bartirome, digging a fingernail into Robinson's finger until he cut it.

Robinson showed the bloodied digit to plate umpire Jerry Neudecker and was awarded first base. He received credit for an RBI and Bartirome received credit for an "assist."

Q The Pirates' batting coach in 1960 was labeled "the nearest thing to a perfect ballplayer" by no less an authority than Ty Cobb. Name him.

A George Sisler, whose official title was Special Assistant to the Manager. Roberto Clemente, who would capture four batting titles in a seven-season span starting in 1961, benefited most from Sisler's tutelage.

The Hall of Fame first baseman was certainly qualified as a hitting instructor: He finished his career (1915-30) with a .340 average—the 14th-best all-time—twice hit above .400, captured a pair of batting titles and set a major league record in 1920 with 257 hits.

Sisler's 1922 season with the St. Louis Browns ranks among the finest ever. He led the American League with a .420 batting average, 134 runs, 246 hits, 18 triples and 51 stolen bases, established an AL record with a 41-game batting streak, knocked in 105 runs and ran away with league MVP honors.

Incidentally, Sisler's baseball coach at the University of Michigan was Branch Rickey, later the Pirates' general manager.

Q Which Pirates Hall of Famer once went an entire season without striking out?

A Lloyd Waner, who did not fan at all in 219 at bats during the 1941 season as a part-time outfielder with the Bucs, Braves and Reds. Remarkably, Waner struck out only 173 times in 18 years as a big leaguer.

A HAIR-RAISING ADVENTURE

I n 1953, Joseph Strouse of DuBois demonstrated his faith in the Pirates—then baseball's worst team—by putting his razor in mothballs.

Strouse resolved to grow a beard. That didn't raise eyebrows so much as the vow that accompanied his decision: Strouse declared he would not shave until the Bucs won the National League pennant.

Some acquaintances called him an incurable optimist; some just called him daft. After all, the Bucs of the early 1950s were downright abysmal, scarcely major league caliber at all. His beard will reach the floor before the Pirates reach the World Series, the critics were convinced.

But seven years later the Bucs brought a pennant to Pittsburgh and relief to the man whose scratchy beard had, by then, grown long and lush. The seven-year itch was history. Strouse could finally take razor to chin and, clean-shaven, cheer on his beloved Bucs in the World Series.

Strouse earned national notoriety in 1960 for his hirsute pursuit, but that was never his intent. He cared about the Pirates, not the publicity.

"He did it for the love of the team," recalled his brother Paul, who resides in DuBois. "He was shy and quiet. He didn't do it to get attention or to be recognized."

Strouse, who died in 1991 only hours after watching the Pirates lose to Atlanta in the playoffs, initially allowed his whiskers to grow for the Clearfield County Centennial celebration in 1953. "But after the Centennial, he went on the 'shave strike' until the Pirates won the pennant," noted the caption accompanying his photo in the Sept. 24, 1960, edition of the *DuBois Courier-Express*. That photo was distributed throughout the United States and Canada by the Associated Press.

"Everybody laughed at him while he grew the beard, but he wasn't gonna shave until the Pirates won it," Paul said. "He was sort of bullheaded. When he made up his mind to do something, nobody could talk him out of it."

Strouse's whiskers measured some nine inches in length when the Bucs clinched the pennant in 1960, their first in 33 years. The beard came off a few days later at his home, without fanfare. A ceremony involving singer Perry Como, a fellow Pirates fan from Canonsburg, had long been planned. But when the time came, Como declined to wield the barber's shears.

"It really broke Joe's heart—they had him revved up with that Perry Como stuff for two years," Paul said. "He was supposed to do it on his television show. But then Perry backed out for some reason. Something about the network."

Backing out was an option Joe Strouse never considered. He made a crazy vow in 1953—crazy because the Pirates of that era were such a laughingstock—and he followed through on it.

When the Bucs finally captured the pennant in 1960, Strouse celebrated with more fervor than most fans. Because Pittsburgh had won, he could lose, at long last, what one writer called "that load off his chin."

Q This pitcher won 82 games with the Pirates, but perhaps his biggest victory came in a Phillies uniform—during the 1980 World Series. Name him.

A Current Bucs broadcaster Bob Walk, who hurled seven innings as the Phils defeated Kansas City 7-6 in Game 1. Walk, 11-7 during the season, was the first rookie pitcher to start a Series opener since Brooklyn's Joe Black in 1952.

He was elected to start almost by default. Manager Dallas Green had used three starting pitchers in the deciding game of the National League

Championship Series against Houston only two nights before. Four consecutive extra-inning games in the NLCS had stretched his staff dangerously thin.

"For Dallas Green, the choice was a simple one," wrote Bruce Keidan of the *Pittsburgh Post-Gazette*. "Either give the ball to Walk or comb the stands seeking applicants for the job. All of Green's remaining arms hung limply from the shoulders of pitchers thoroughly worn out during the League Championship Series."

Walk yielded early two-run homers to Amos Otis and Willie Mays Aikens, but he settled down and his teammates ultimately wiped out the 4-0 deficit and grabbed the lead. Walk wound up as the second Phillies pitcher to record a World Series victory. The first? Hall of Famer Grover Cleveland Alexander, way back in 1915.

"Last year at this time I was working in a gas station in Newhall, Calif.," said Walk, marveling at the dizzying turn of events. "I just pumped gas, changed oil, did tuneups, the usual stuff. I don't think I'm going back."

Q When this player joined the Pirates, the single-season franchise record for stolen bases was 63. He eventually raised it to 96, ironically in a year when that total wasn't even sufficient to lead the league. Name him.

A Omar Moreno, who lost out to Montreal's Ron LeFlore in the 1980 stolen base race—by one.

Moreno arrived in Pittsburgh in 1975, 59 years after Max Carey set a modern team record with 63 steals. Frank Taveras eclipsed Carey's mark with 70 stolen bases in 1977, but Moreno erased Taveras' name from the books with 71 steals a year later. He improved to 77 stolen bases in 1979 and then established the current club record of 96 in 1980—along with a team mark for times caught stealing (33).

The all-time Pirates steals standard was held for 91 years by Billy Sunday, who swiped 71 bases in 1888. Of course, Sunday's total is somewhat spurious in view of 19th-century scoring rules: Players were often credited with thefts if they moved up on a fly ball or a grounder or took an extra base on a teammate's hit.

By the way, Moreno's total of 96 steals ranks 10th in the modern era, tied with Ty Cobb.

Q Which one-time Pirate said the following: "I was not successful as a ballplayer, as it was a game of skill"?

A Casey Stengel, who was guilty of extreme modesty.

"The Ol' Professor" hit .284 in a 14-year career as an outfielder with four National League clubs. He spent two of those seasons with the Pirates (1918-19).

Stengel was at his best in the postseason. He batted a sizzling .393 in three World Series appearances for the Dodgers (1916) and Giants (1922, 1923) and slugged two game-winning home runs against the Yankees—the team he'd manage to unprecedented heights—in the 1923 Fall Classic.

Incidentally, Stengel offered the above appraisal of his ability during a 1958 Senate hearing investigating baseball's exemption from anti-trust restraints. Chairman Estes Kefauver asked him to make a preliminary statement regarding his background in the game, never imagining Stengel would ramble on and on.

Q Which Pirates shortstop once had his wife arrested?

A Willie Kuehne, who started for the Bucs' first team in 1887.

Kuehne ordered the arrest of his wife for "unpleasant demonstrations." The *Pittsburgh Post* reported that, while her husband was absent on a road trip, Mrs. Kuehne's conduct "was of the most questionable kind."

Kuehne spent three seasons with the Pirates (1887-1889). He also played for Pittsburgh's American Association and Players League clubs.

Q Elmer Jacobs worked overtime in relief on Aug. 22, 1917, pitching more innings than anyone ever has coming out of the Pirates' bullpen. Just how long did Jacobs labor?

A Sixteen and two-thirds innings. Jacobs entered in the sixth inning of a 22-inning marathon at Brooklyn and went the rest of the way, absorbing a 6-5 loss even though he yielded but one run.

Wrote Edward F. Balinger in the *Pittsburgh Post*, "Elmer's work was brilliant all the way and on many occasions the crowd accorded him rounds of well-deserved applause."

And these were Dodgers fans, remember.

Q Which Pirate was the oldest player in history to win an MVP award?

A Willie "Pops" Stargell in 1979, at the age of 38.

Q Which current Pirate tied a national record for the longest batting streak during his high school days?

A Catcher Jason Kendall, who hit safely in 43 consecutive games spanning his junior and senior years at Torrance (Calif.) High School to equal the National Federation of State and High School Associations mark set in 1980 by Tom Imhoff of Lansing Kee (Iowa) High School.

The current record of 51 is shared by Stan Brown of Walton Cass (Ind.) High and Shawn Gallagher of Wilmington New Hanover (N.C.) High. Kendall and Imhoff rank right behind Brown and Gallagher on the all-time list.

"The amazing thing about his streak, teams didn't want to pitch to him," said Don Nicholson, then a Torrance assistant coach. "It got to the point where he was walked intentionally one or two times a game, but he still was able to keep it alive."

Kendall hit .549 (45-for-82) as a senior at Torrance, with three home runs, 39 RBIs and 21 stolen bases. He passed on a scholarship offer by San Diego State to sign with the Bucs, who selected him with their first pick (23rd overall) in the 1992 free-agent draft.

Q Which entertainment megastar smashed two batting practice home runs after joining the Pirates for pre-game drills on Sept. 13, 1998?

A Country singer Garth Brooks, who took BP and shagged flies before a game against the Phillies at Veterans Stadium. Brooks, who has won 16 Academy of Country Music awards, 13 American Music Awards, two Grammys and sold 95 million albums—more than any other solo artist in American music history—was in Philadelphia for a series of concerts.

"Garth is a big Pirates fan," said club owner Kevin McClatchy. "His favorite player was Roberto Clemente. He just wanted the opportunity to take batting practice. I think the players have had fun with it. It's all been very low key."

The switch-hitting Brooks, a high school javelin champion in his native Oklahoma—he went to Oklahoma State on a track scholarship—smacked home runs from each side of the plate.

Brooks trained in Arizona with the San Diego Padres this spring, partly to jump-start contributions to his Touch 'Em All Foundation, which benefits children's charities.

Q Tom Greenwade of the Yankees had a major impact on the 1960 World Series, even though he didn't play, manage or coach. What did he do?

A Greenwade, a Yankees scout, discovered both Series center fielders—Mickey Mantle and Bill Virdon. Mantle was a sandlot standout in his native Oklahoma, Virdon in neighboring Missouri.

Both players starred in the 1960 Series. Mantle batted .400, slugged three home runs and drove in 11 runs. Virdon, who spent four seasons in the Yankees' minor league system, saved two Pittsburgh victories with spectacular catches.

Q Who was the last Pirates pitcher to enjoy back-to-back 20-win seasons?

A Rip Sewell in 1943 (21-9) and 1944 (21-12). Those were the only 20-win seasons of his career.

MISDIRECTION PLAY

T he *Chicago Tribune* labeled Cubs pitcher Jimmy St. Vrain "the poorest hitter in the league" in 1902. It was his futility at the plate that inspired a slapstick sequence during an April 27 game against the Pirates at West Side Grounds.

Chicago manager Frank Selee jokingly suggested to the right-handed hitting St. Vrain that he might have better luck turning around and batting from the opposite side. St. Vrain assumed Selee was serious and stepped in against Deacon Phillippe as a left-hander. He then stunned everyone—but mostly himself—by making contact. That's when St. Vrain *really* got turned around.

"He tapped a slow roller to Honus Wagner at shortstop and took off as fast as he could go," Cubs outfielder Davy Jones recalled years later. "But instead of running to first base, he headed for third. Oh, my God, what bedlam! Everybody yelling and screaming at poor Jimmy as he raced to third base, head down, spikes flying, determined to get there ahead of the throw."

Wagner, who fielded the grounder, was momentarily frozen by the sight of St. Vrain dashing madly in the wrong direction.

"I'm standing there with the ball in my hand looking at this guy running from home to third and for an instant there I swear I didn't know *where* to throw the damn ball," Wagner said. "And when I finally did throw to first, I wasn't at all sure it was the right thing to do."

Q Which Pirate roomed with future Denver Broncos quarterback John Elway while both were students at Stanford?

A Third baseman Steve Buechele, who spent parts of the 1991 and 1992 seasons in Pittsburgh. Both played baseball at Stanford—Buechele from 1980 to 1982, Elway during the 1980 and 1981 seasons.

Elway spent one season as a minor league outfielder with the Yankees' Class A Oneonta, N.Y., farm club before deciding to earn his livelihood throwing footballs, not baseballs.

Buechele wrapped up his major league career in 1995. Elway wrapped up his NFL career after leading the Broncos to victory in Super Bowl XXXIII on Jan. 31.

Q Which Pirate holds the National League record for most home runs hit by a player in his final season?

A Hank Greenberg, who slugged 25 homers in 1947, his only year in Pittsburgh. That ranks Greenberg third on the all-time list. Oakland's Dave Kingman set the major league mark with 35 in 1986, eclipsing the old record of 29 established by Ted Williams of the Red Sox in 1960.

Q One of the most improbable comebacks in Pirates history occurred on May 3, 1985, during a 16-2 victory over Los Angeles at Three Rivers Stadium. What happened that night?

A Bob Prince returned with great fanfare to the KDKA broadcast booth, 10 years after his unpopular dismissal. His voice quavering and his diction impaired by recent oral surgery, Prince nevertheless showed he still had his old magic.

The Bucs erupted for nine runs in the fourth—the very inning Prince began his play-by-play duties—en route to their most lopsided victory since a 22-0 rout of the Cubs on Sept. 16, 1975, a span of 1,430 games. To borrow a phrase, how sweet it was.

A crowd of 17,628 rose to its feet and chants of "Gunner, Gunner" reverberated throughout Three Rivers when Prince appeared in the booth. He rained his trademark Green Weenies on the fans below and then described, with unabashed glee, the nine-run explosion that sealed the Dodgers' fate.

Was the power of Prince's magical talisman, which had been recharging for a decade, responsible for the outburst? He scoffed at the notion while addressing the media following his two-inning stint.

"If you think that happened because of me," Prince said, "you can put away all your pens and pencils and microphones and we can form a cult together."

Still, an inexplicable force seemed to emanate from the KDKA booth. The last-place Pirates played like champions in Prince's presence, as two-run singles by Tony Pena, Sixto Lezcano and Bill Almon fueled their fourth-inning uprising.

Manager Chuck Tanner welcomed the deluge of runs—and Prince's return.

"Bob Prince is an institution in Pittsburgh," Tanner said. "It's great to have him back."

Prince was rehired in mid-April, not long after surgery to remove a cancerous tumor from his mouth. At a press conference to announce his return, Prince—his voice choked with emotion—said, "You've given me back the thing in the world that I love most, besides my family."

Sadly, Prince worked but three games before ill health forced him from the booth for good. He died on June 10, only 38 days after his triumphant return to Three Rivers Stadium.

Of the dozens of eulogies spoken in his behalf, none capsulized Prince's hold on a city better than these simple words from general manager Joe L. Brown: "To many, he *was* the Pittsburgh Pirates."

Q Name the scout whose work helped place the Pirates at the forefront as far as recruiting prospects from talent-rich Latin America.

A Howie Haak, who spent 38 years with the Bucs before leaving in 1988 to take a scouting position with Houston. Haak discovered dozens of gems in Latin America at a time when many major league teams evinced little interest in the area.

Among his finds: Manny Sanguillen, Rennie Stennett and Omar Moreno of Panama, Tony Pena of the Dominican Republic and Al McBean of the Virgin Islands, who showed up at a tryout wearing a camera around his neck and street shoes on his feet.

Haak also encouraged the Pirates to draft Roberto Clemente after general manager Branch Rickey dispatched him on a 1954 scouting trip to Montreal, where Clemente was playing for Brooklyn's top farm club.

Said former Pittsburgh GM Harding Peterson, "One statement would sum up everything: The Pirates would not have been as good if it wasn't for Howie."

Q Which Pirates pitcher sported the longest full name in major league history?

A Cal McLish, who was christened Calvin Coolidge Julius Caesar Tuskahoma McLish. That's a total of six names and 41 letters.

McLish once explained that, because his father was not involved in naming his first six children, he "caught up" with his seventh. He was named for the president at the time of his birth, a Roman emperor and an Indian chief.

"Being part Indian, I guess he felt he had to get an Indian name in there somewhere," McLish said. "I've always claimed he had to be in the firewater to give a kid a name like that."

McLish, who spent 15 seasons in the majors, pitched briefly for the Pirates in 1947 and 1948.

Q What did Lloyd and Paul Waner accomplish on Sept. 15, 1938, that had never been done before and hasn't been duplicated since?

A They became the only brothers in major league history to slug back-to-back home runs, connecting against Cliff Melton of the Giants at the Polo Grounds. Lloyd hit a two-run homer in the fifth inning and Paul followed with a solo shot.

Lloyd Waner's homer was his last in the big leagues, even though he didn't retire until after the 1945 season.

Q Who was the first Pirate to hit at least 20 home runs and steal at least 20 bases in the same season?

A A player from way back? Hardly. Dave Parker became the Bucs' first 20-20 man in 1978 (30 home runs, 20 steals) and then repeated his feat in 1979 (25-20).

Barry Bonds (25-32) and Andy Van Slyke (21-34) gave Pittsburgh its first 20-20 tandem eight years later. Bonds recorded four 20-20 seasons, the most in franchise history.

Q What are the odds of two brothers winding up as major league relief pitchers? Not as remote as you might think, given that this former Pirates hurler has nearly 40 siblings. Name him.

A Ravelo Manzanillo, who joined the Bucs in 1994. He and Josias, a reliever for the Mets, became the first brothers in big league history to record saves on the same date: June 30, 1994.

Demetrio Manzanillo fathered 38 children, though not by the same woman (as if *that* needed to be pointed out). The gender breakdown is also remarkable, considering the mathematical odds against it: 32 boys, six girls.

Q This Pirate was the only pitcher to complete a low-hit game (defin. as a no-hitter, one-hitter or two-hitter) in a span of 27 World Series. Name him.

A Nellie Briles, who two-hit the Baltimore Orioles in a 4-0 victory on Oct. 14, 1971, to give the Bucs a three games-to-two lead in the Series. That was the only complete game low-hitter between 1967, when Boston's Jim Lonborg one-hit the Cardinals in Game 2, and 1995, when Atlanta's Greg Maddux two-hit the Indians in Game 1.

Until Briles' masterful effort at Three Rivers Stadium, Deacon Phillippe held the team record for fewest hits allowed in a complete game World Series effort. Phillippe hurled a four-hitter en route to a 4-2 victory over Boston in Game 3 of the 1903 Fall Classic.

Q The *Pittsburgh Press* polled its readers to select an all-time Pirates team in 1987, the 100th anniversary of the franchise. Which player received the highest percentage of votes?

A Outfielder Roberto Clemente, with 96 percent.

The rest of the team, in order of percentage of votes received: second baseman Bill Mazeroski (88), third baseman Pie Traynor (79), first baseman Willie Stargell (78), shortstop Honus Wagner (74), relief pitcher Elroy Face (73), outfielders Paul Waner (56) and Ralph Kiner (55), left-handed pitcher Harvey Haddix (46), right-handed pitcher Vernon Law (44) and catcher Manny Sanguillen (33).

Danny Murtaugh was selected as the manager with 79 percent of the vote.